W9-CPE-606

The Innovator's Path

How Individuals, Teams, and Organizations Can Make Innovation Business-as-Usual

Madge M. Meyer

WILEY

Library of Congress Cataloging-in-Publication Data:
Meyer, Madge M.,
  The innovator's path : how individuals, teams, and organizations can make innovation business-as-usual / Madge M. Meyer.
       pages cm
  Includes index.
  ISBN 978-1-118-53732-9 (cloth); ISBN 978-1-118-56989-4 (ebk);
ISBN 978-1-118-56985-6 (ebk)   1. Leadership.   2. Listening.   3. Strategic planning.
4. Industrial management–Technological innovations.   I. Title.
  HD57.7.M4896 2013
  658.4'063–dc23

                                                   2013013980

Printed in the United States of America

10 9 8 7 6 5 4 3 2 1

This book is dedicated to my parents,
Nai Ying Chang Mao and Pei Ching Mao;
My husband, Werner, and our dearest daughter, Michele;
My brother, Michael, and sisters, Margo, Marjorie, and Marsha.

Contents

Foreword

As I read Madge Meyer's book *The Innovator's Path*, I could not help but think about my first week at my new job at State Street Bank. I had been working for a competitor for twenty years where I watched as State Street built an unassailable franchise serving the mutual fund industry. Luckily, after twenty years of competing against State Street, I had an opportunity to join the company and manage its largest business, the mutual funds servicing business. That first week told me why they had been consistently successful all those years, and why I had such difficulty competing against them.

Very early during that first week I had many conversations with the senior officials of the company. One of them took me aside and said, "You need to know one thing, you are not working for a bank, you are working for an IT company disguised as a bank." It became very clear to me why I had such difficulty competing against State Street. I had been working for a bank that thought of itself as a bank and used IT as a "necessary evil."

State Street very early on figured out what Madge writes about in her book—making innovation business-as-usual. In today's fast-paced, high-tech world, this approach is more important than ever.

Any industry using technology, and I would suggest that almost all do, may want to think of itself as an IT company disguised as whatever it is they do—at least when it comes to innovation.

Later during that first week, a young, aggressive salesperson bounded into my office saying he needed my support for a new product, that in his words, "would revolutionize the mutual funds world, and we had to be the first to do this and seize first mover advantage." He was working with our asset management group, State Street Global Advisors (SSGA), and the American Stock Exchange to develop a mutual fund that could be traded on a stock exchange. The cost advantage would be significant, and therefore, the advisory fee charged would be far less than traditional mutual funds, among the many advantages of such a product. These products were to be known as exchange-traded funds or ETFs. This was 1991, and as the world now knows, State Street offered the first ETF in early 1993, called the Standard and Poor's Depository Receipt, or SPDR, which is today still the largest ETF in the world, within an investment category that has, in fact, revolutionized the mutual funds industry.

So what type of environment exists within a firm that allows an idea like the ETF to be created? That gives an individual the freedom to marshal resources to address a current customer's idea? That would normally consider the idea a threat to the largest and most profitable business of the company, the mutual fund servicing business? How does that idea not get killed somewhere in the normal corporate process of annual budgets, expense cutbacks, organizational jealousies, and the like? The answers, I believe, can be found in Madge's book. Yes, it is about *making innovation business-as-usual*. But how does that happen? There has to be a discipline and a simple-to-understand methodology if it is to be inculcated within a large organization and adopted as a way of life for so many. It obviously starts with what the organization thinks it is. The innovation doesn't always have to come from IT. It just happens that IT creates a great deal of innovation. Process change, regulatory change, environment, geography, customer needs, and many other things can facilitate innovation.

What Madge Meyer has done in her book is use a simple, common-sense approach to following through with the good idea that all too often dies a premature death. Focusing on the eight disciplines, she carefully describes a set of critical skills for turning a good idea into reality and, many times, into competitive advantage. If you apply them to my ETF example, you will see how practical the discipline is, and how effective it can be.

My aggressive salesperson, long before bringing this idea back to management, spent significant time LISTENING to the customer, the American Stock Exchange, and SSgA, making sure in his mind that it was viable and worth fighting for. He demonstrated his LEADERSHIP by aligning the key stakeholders, including me, to support this vision, which he saw was POSITIONED to succeed. This salesperson needed others to make the product a reality, so he CONNECTED with IT, mutual funds operations, legal, and so on—as Madge says, no one innovates alone. This salesperson was COMMITED to this idea. Courage is needed to put one's career on the line for a new idea. An innovative organization must allow failures to occur, or else others will not try. This salesperson, being a salesperson, PROMOTED the idea throughout the organization, selling it internally just as he would sell a service to a customer. This salesperson demonstrated perseverance and EXECUTED over a sustained period of time. And we didn't stop there. We continue even today to EVOLVE this game-changing innovation.

The best way I can explain it is, without these disciplines, it does not happen. This is why Madge Meyer's book needs to be read, not just by CEOs and other senior managers, but by all those numerous facilitators within the corporate hierarchy who have the power to kill or proceed with an idea. It is only when more people within an organization are employing these disciplines, than are not, that an organization will become truly innovative.

Ron Logue
Chairman and CEO (retired)
State Street Corporation

Preface

I speak to audiences all over the world about a subject I am most passionate about: *innovation*. Sometimes I look out at auditoriums full of senior executives, and other times I find myself speaking to young professionals or students. But no matter who is in the audience, I am always happy to see that my message has been accepted when I see a line of people forming at the front of the room to speak with me. Some of these people just want to shake my hand and tell me that they've enjoyed my talk. Others have questions or comments, and given the number of speeches I make, it is not unusual for some to tell me this is not the first time they've heard me. Those who have heard me speak before often want to tell me how they've put my recommendations to use, and they are eager to share their stories. Oftentimes at least one person in line tells me: "You should write a book, Madge. There are so many people and companies out there who could use your advice."

Well, I finally took that advice, and this book is the result. I call it *The Innovator's Path*—not because I believe we must all follow the exact same route to innovation; we don't. Quite the contrary: Each of us must create our own way forward. Yet it is also true that, no matter what path we take, most of us will encounter similar challenges as we try to innovate, including the beliefs, attitudes, and behaviors of our colleagues and our managers.

I am happy to say that over the years I have found certain fundamental ways of making innovation happen—*disciplines*, I call them—that can be used to make our path more smooth and effective. Those disciplines, and the techniques that derive from them, can be used by individuals, teams, and even entire organizations. Together they form the heart of my book.

My disciplines are tried and true, fashioned and fine-tuned during my decades-long career in executive leadership positions at IBM, Merrill Lynch, and lastly at State Street, where I served as executive vice president, chief innovation officer & technology fellow. At each of these great companies, I took on roles of increasing responsibility in global technology and innovation, and my teams achieved a distinguished record of accomplishment, winning 32 industry awards over the last decade. Now I would like to share my many years of diverse experiences and lessons learned in the chapters of this book.

超越創新

There is no single Chinese character for the word "innovation." Instead, I have used the characters on the first page of this book—pronounced *Chāoyuè Chuangxin*—to convey the essence of *The Innovator's Path*, and to represent my approach to innovation.

Both of the first two characters are built around the same radical (or root), 走 *zou*, dipping tone, which depending on its context can mean, among many other things, *to go*, *to leave*, or *to go along*.

The first, 超 *chāo*, level tone, represents a human being going forward—or better still, going *beyond* his or her present position.

The second character, 越, *yuè*, falling tone, signifies the continual act of excelling or overtaking—that is, a process in constant motion. Together, 超 and 越 reinforce one another, creating the simultaneous sense of *ongoing* and *going beyond*.

The third character, 創, *chuàng*, means "to carve out." The right side of the character is the "particle," or root form of the word "knife." Thousands of years ago characters were carved on oracle bones with a knife or sharp implement, and thus "knife" carries with it the sense of "to originate, to make real, to cause to exist." The left side of the character consists of 倉, *cang*, first tone, meaning "warehouse," derived from the term for "food," 食 *si*, first tone.

The fourth character, 新 *xin*, is an ancient character and means "new" in the sense of "that which has not yet emerged." On the right side is the pictograph for axe, 斤 *jin*, supplying a pronunciation guide. On the left is the term for hardship, 辛 *xin*. For that reason, I prefer to use the compound word *Chuangxin* because of its positive, forward-looking meaning.

Throughout my life, and over the course of my corporate career, I have found that those individuals capable of blazing a trail to innovation share several basic character traits. They are usually very determined and very willing to work exceptionally hard to achieve the goals they believe in. They are also surprisingly open to alternatives and exhibit the willingness to try a variety of ways to reach their goals as new information and new ideas come to light. Indeed, most innovators share yet another character trait: They are also willing to shed old assumptions and adopt new and even unusual approaches *if* they believe it will speed their progress.

On the other hand, I've watched people go to extraordinary lengths to hold on to the things they are used to and that they value, resisting change even when change has become the only way to survive in a constantly mutating world. Resistance to change is certainly not hard to understand. Many of us prefer the familiarity and security of our well-understood, proven ways. We may avoid what is untested or unproven, perhaps because we believe that it will be too difficult for us or that we won't be good at it.

Rapid change, though, has become the new normal in life and in work. There is simply no way to avoid it. In fact, why would we want to avoid it? Change can be exciting and life-changing in a positive sense! That's really the reason I decided to write this book. The business world has become a world of creating, innovating, and forging ahead. If we don't do this, our competitors surely will. I am determined to teach as many people as I can how to incorporate this new reality into their day-to-day practices. I hope my book will inspire readers to make innovation part of their new business-as-usual. We simply cannot afford to rest on our laurels. We need to be creative and innovative and push the boundaries of whatever business or industry we serve. But most of us don't walk around thinking we are the most brilliant, innovative people around. How are we and our organizations supposed to thrive in this new world if we are merely smart people who are good at our jobs? Nathan Myhrvold, the celebrated inventor and entrepreneur who was formerly chief technology officer at Microsoft, has offered some interesting insights into the nature of the innovative organization and some hope for those of us who may not consider "creativity" one of our top traits:

> Being creative is some weird mixture of things that you learn and things that are innate in you. It's hard for a company to be creative, and it's hard for many individuals to be creative, but you can have an innovative company even if not everybody in the company is creative. The trick is that you really have to set out to be innovative. A lot of companies just wait around for innovation to happen to them. But I think, as in most things in life, including innovation, if you want it to occur, you should actively seek it. Eureka moments occur, but they occur more often to people who are trying to solve a problem, not to people who are not.

★ ★ ★

I was born in Shanghai, China, and then moved to Hong Kong as a teenager. My upbringing, my family life, my exposure to the culture of my native country has influenced me in many profound ways, of course. But interestingly, it has also taught me many lessons that I have applied to my career. I thought my readers would be interested in this cross-cultural phenomenon, so I have included some anecdotes from my personal life that have direct relevance or direct application to the subject of innovation. In addition, I have reproduced traditional Chinese ideograms in each chapter that represent and help describe and explain the terminology I have chosen for each of the eight disciplines of innovation.

When I began planning this book, I reached out to many leaders in industry, government, education, and the military who have world-class reputations as innovators. I sought their personal views on a variety of subjects involving their experiences as innovators and leaders. I am pleased and deeply honored by the thoughtful responses they have provided to me. Throughout these pages, readers will find observations and advice from these leaders, inventors and innovators, in their own words, adding a depth and richness to the book that I could have never achieved on my own.

In my Introduction, I define what I mean by the word *innovation* and introduce in depth the eight disciplines I've used to advance innovation over the course of my career and at the companies I've worked. My greatest pleasure has always come from helping colleagues and employees chart their own paths to innovation—and I have to admit, not letting them rest on their laurels but leading them to the next innovation path. Nothing excites me more. It is my hope that the book will show my readers how they can walk (or run!) along their own paths to innovation and change.

So let's get started!

Acknowledgments

The first person I want to thank is my extremely dedicated and talented chief-of-staff for the past decade at State Street, Marcy Wintrub. Marcy is a passionate leader of organizational change. She quickly saw the value of the disciplines I practice and has always encouraged me to share them with others. She is a gifted communicator and writer who helped immeasurably and generously to shape and deliver my message. Without Marcy, this would not be the same book.

I am indebted to my brother, Michael Mao, for the illuminating Chinese references. Michael has a B.A. from Princeton University in Oriental Studies and an M.A. from Harvard University in East Asian Languages and Civilizations.

I thank my sisters, Margo and Marjorie, for their autobiographical contributions and ongoing support as well.

I would like to express my heartfelt appreciation to the great leaders and innovators who graciously and generously provided words of wisdom to share with my readers. They are in alphabetical order: Dr. Tenley Albright, Deborah Ancona, Marc Andreessen, Dr. Eugene Chan, Gerald Chertavian, Dean Kamen, Tarkan Maner, Tom Mendoza, Admiral Michael Mullen, Nathan Myhrvold, Sam Palmisano, Jim

Phalen, Linda Sanford, John Swainson, John Thompson, and Ming Tsai. I have learned so much from them and continue to benefit from their mentoring, friendship, and partnership. Their accomplishments are evidence of their principles at work. I thank each of them for their tremendous support, generosity, mentoring, and contributions to this book. It is my great good fortune to have enjoyed such incredible support and friendship!

I would like to highlight my special gratitude to Jim Phalen for his continual encouragement and enduring support during this journey.

I extend my deep gratitude to Ron Logue for contributing his Foreword to my book and for his visionary leadership during our time together at State Street. Ron inspired innovation by painting a clear picture of the future, upholding high standards of achievement, and personally recognizing those who attained them.

I would like to thank Duane Barton, Ellie Carlough, Elaine Doherty, Gregory Golden, David Knies, Anna Manville, Cathy Minehan, Dr. Randy O'Rear, Lorna Rankin, Howard Rubin, Lenny Teng, and Andrew Xue for their invaluable support.

I would like to thank Dave Conti for his talented and skillful editing and writing, done in a short timeframe, and thereby helping to accurately articulate my voice and message.

I would like to thank my agent, Joelle Delbourgo, for her assistance all along this writing journey.

I would like to thank State Street's executive leadership team for their personal encouragement and commitment to making innovation business-as-usual.

I would like to thank State Street's Global Infrastructure Services and Innovation Office—the senior managers who worked for me directly, my entire management team, and every staff member—for their many achievements, only some of which I have been able to include here. I would also like to thank the many partners who contributed so greatly to our success.

I would like to say thank you to all those who provided their support and encouragement throughout this process.

Last, but not least, are all the leaders I have worked for over the years. I thank all of you for your teaching, coaching, and support.

Author's Note

Regarding the Chinese Ideograms That Appear in This Book

The ideograms for the eight disciplines in this book would make sense to all those who have learned Chinese characters in the traditional way. Simplified Chinese characters no longer contain some of these thousand-year-old concepts which have been embedded or have grown out of the Chinese language.

Chinese Title	超越創新	Chāoyuè Chuangxin (Beyond Innovation)
Innovation	創新軟力	Chuangxin Ruanli
Discipline	技巧	Jì Qiǎo
Listen	聽	Ting
Lead	領	Ling
Position	計	Jì
Promote	提	Ti
Connect	連	Lian
Commit	承	Cheng
Execute	行	Xing
Evolve	變	Bian

Whenever a Chinese character appears, it is followed by a Romanization according to the pinyin system, now officially used worldwide. It is not a phonetic system, nor a strict Romanization system. It uses the Roman alphabet to stand for sounds or groups of sounds that exist in China but perhaps not elsewhere. Certain letters deemed "underused" were assigned to stand for a group of sounds. For example, the underused letter "x" was drafted to stand for "hs," while underused "q" takes on the burden to stand for "ch." Economy is a virtue. When language is involved, clarity is perhaps more important than economy. Throughout the work, traditional Chinese characters are used. Traditional Chinese characters evolved over thousands of years from inscriptions with sharp implements onto oracle bones. These evolved into slightly more abstract or angular forms, but remain closer to the original pictures. In time, ideas were represented by ideographs. Pictographs and ideographs combined to form actions or objects which cannot be drawn. For readers who wish to see what the simplified characters may be, please use Google, which tends to include more modern renditions of meaning as well.

Most of the characters used are contained within Zhongwen.com, Guoyuromaji jiten, and Matthews Dictionary.

Some of the basic items are simple pictographs or slightly more sophisticated ideographs. These begin to combine to form more sophisticated ideas; by the time of Confucius (551–479 BCE), a gentleman's canon of books to study already consisted of five classics and the four books. These continued to be the curriculum for scholars throughout Imperial China for two thousand years.

超越創新

Introduction

Innovation and the Eight Disciplines

I often get a quizzical look when I ask, "Are you an innovator?"
Some people answer right away, but most have to think about it. There are several reasons why it can be a difficult question to answer. First of all, innovators are generally recognized after the fact, not *while* they are innovating. For example, in 2007, Sal Khan was a hedge fund manager creating YouTube videos for his cousin in his spare time. Five years later, after founding Khan Academy, his free online school where lessons are taught via video lectures, he was named by *Time* magazine as one of the 100 most influential people in the world.

Sal Khan's achievement is a perfect example of what Marc Andreessen, the Internet visionary and co-founder and partner of the venture capital firm Andreessen Horowitz, says in describing how innovation happens: "Companies innovate by fostering a culture that strives to identify, embrace, and reward change. The idea that seems trivial today could be game changing tomorrow."

Like Sal, most innovators are people who put their energy, intellect, and passion into achieving particular goals or solving specific problems.

1

Like Sal, a few come up with the right solution in the right place at the right time, striking such a chord that they end up impacting an entire industry or culture or world. Unlike Sal, however, most innovators don't quite change the world, yet their solutions can still create significant value, at a smaller scale.

There's a second reason why my question is difficult for many people to answer. And that's because there's no universally accepted definition for *innovator*, or for what an innovation is.

Defining Innovation

For the purposes of this book, I suggest we think of innovation, specifically business innovation, very broadly. I like to define it as any new idea or solution that creates business value and increases competitive advantage. It can be a new or different process, product, service, strategy . . . anything, as long as it creates value and increases competitive advantage. I also suggest we think of a business innovator as anyone who is developing or adopting a new idea or solution in order to accomplish these ends.

I know there are people who will see this definition as too broad, too all-encompassing. And I understand why. Casting such a wide net somewhat diminishes the exceptional achievements of those who have brought about truly revolutionary change. However, that is a very exclusive club, and their achievements are captured elsewhere. I'm writing this book for a different purpose: My focus is not on the nature of radical, game-changing ideas and solutions, but rather on creating business value and increasing competitive advantage by doing things differently and better. Sometimes that means radical game-changing ideas, sometimes it means simple yet meaningful change, and generally it falls somewhere in between.

Let me give you an example from my own experience.

Making Innovation Business-as-Usual

When I was hired by State Street Corporation, one of the world's leading investment service firms, the company was already in the midst of unprecedented global expansion and preparing for even more. In Europe and Asia-Pacific, State Street was growing faster than the market itself. The company was also transforming its operating model and centralizing certain business processes in multiple global locations. As the head of State Street's global infrastructure services group, one of my first major initiatives was to overhaul the company's entire network to provide the foundation for a series of innovative solutions. Here, though, I want to focus in on a specific innovation that we developed to solve a particularly vexing problem.

Due to the nature of State Street's business, we cannot tolerate time delays as our data travels from one point to another, so we historically built local data centers in buildings located near our users. As a result, State Street had a very large number of these data centers and communications rooms, in various sizes, scattered around the world. You can imagine how expensive it was to build, equip, manage, and maintain these data centers. When State Street began to rapidly expand globally, we experienced increasing challenges trying to secure suitable locations, preparing buildings, installing our equipment, and getting everything online in time for use.

A large part of State Street's growth strategy was the acquisition of other companies in Europe and Asia. Acquisitions have very tight, nonnegotiable timeframes for change of control. They are also predicated on specific cost-saving models. I knew we needed an alternative solution if we were going to continue meeting business requirements involving deadlines and cost savings.

I challenged my team, telling them that we were no longer going to replicate individual data centers. At first, some members of the team were concerned that a new approach might itself jeopardize our ability to meet business expectations and timetables. However, a heart-to-heart discussion along with a close look at the facts made the case that the old ways would not work for much longer. Our changing and growing company needed a new kind of support from us, and needed it quickly. My team took on the challenge, and we all got busy looking for a solution.

At that time, a new technology called a network acceleration device was just being developed. We recognized that if it worked well, it could reduce network delays enough to allow employees in these new offices to access their data remotely from regional and enterprise data centers, rather than local ones. It would have to work so well that these employees would not even notice the difference.

Network accelerator technology was so new at that time that our network team had just started testing it and thought it would take another six months before we could implement it. That was not good enough. Our New Business Integration (NBI) team had a tight deadline to meet for a critical business initiative, and I didn't want another local data center. So, I told the NBI team that we had to take on some risk: We would go ahead and install the network accelerators—which were not quite proven—at the site. If it worked, the problem was solved. If it didn't . . . well, we would have to build a new data center at the site as quickly as we could.

Once the plan was set, we met with the firm that was developing the accelerator technology and asked them to provide their best support. They sent their top engineer to our remote location, and he worked side-by-side with our own team. Remarkably, they got the network accelerators installed and working beautifully. Response times were the same as for data centers situated locally. The team then focused on integrating this new technology with other advanced network, server, and desktop virtualization technologies to develop an end-to-end solution. Within weeks we had an entirely new way to support real-time global business processing without requiring IT infrastructure (including servers, storage, e-mail, and backup) at local offices. The solution was so ground-breaking that we even acquired a registered trademark—"Zero Footprint, Maximum Impact"™—and won several industry awards for our innovative solution.

But the most important part of the story is not what we did or how we did it or even how innovative it was. It's the impact that our solution had. To the end-users, of course, the impact was invisible. In fact, that was our goal! In the infrastructure domain, we inherently understand that the less they notice us, the better. To the business, however, the impact was substantial and strategic.

As one might expect, the most visible impact was a dramatic reduction in technology expenses associated with business growth. Rather than having to provision every small office with a specially outfitted room filled with servers and storage, we could leverage existing data centers and equipment. In addition to avoiding costs, this allowed us to greatly reduce the lead-time and staff-effort normally required to prepare new offices or integrate acquired ones. By reducing costs and lead-time, we also reduced project risk for the business, especially for deadline-driven acquisitions.

The benefits went even beyond individual projects. The centralization of infrastructure and application data within regional data centers brought about greater control and resiliency. It eliminated downtime for maintenance and ushered in immediate recovery for local offices, significantly improving business continuity, an increasingly important requirement for operating in a global economy. And it ensured that effective management, security, retention, and other key business controls would be in place, addressing the customary challenges brought on by significant growth.

Soon afterward, this strategic solution became State Street's standard operating model, and the company has continued to reap the strategic benefits for many years. Our work created a brand new and valuable competitive advantage for the company and made a major contribution to rapid business growth and enduring global success.

We had taken a calculated risk—integrating new and unproven technology into a larger business solution. And it paid off. Our team was positively thrilled with our collaborative triumph, and the industry recognition we received became a major milestone in everyone's personal careers. My favorite part of the story, though, is the motto the team repeated every time we were congratulated for our efforts: "It's just another day!"

That's what this book is about: making innovation business-as-usual.

Different Contexts

Since my background and experience has been with large corporations, most of the material you will find in this book has also been written in that context. However, in developing the book, I was very fortunate to have received input from many renowned innovators and prominent executives with an extraordinary range of experiences. If I wasn't convinced before, I certainly am now: There are many more similarities than differences when it comes to introducing something new, regardless of the context in which we are operating.

My background has also included technology and management. I began my career as an IBM scientific programmer assigned to NASA, programming the onboard computer for the last three Gemini space flights. Over the years, I moved into IT (information technology) infrastructure, which soon became my specialty. As I mentioned, the best infrastructure is the least noticed infrastructure. Often, the role of infrastructure becomes most visible when it's not working. For example, prior to Superbowl XLVII, how many football fans ever gave a moment's thought to stadium lighting?

I bring up my background in IT infrastructure because it has lessons to offer aspiring innovators in many different fields. Innovation is challenging in IT infrastructure for several reasons. First, except to a small segment of the population, there's nothing "cool" about infrastructure. In most corporations, there's not much interest, funding, or support for good infrastructure ideas when everything is running smoothly. Generally, the much "cooler" revenue-generating ideas get the most attention. And by the time things conveniently ignored in the existing underlying infrastructure are not running smoothly, well, it's too late. We're suddenly getting the wrong kind of attention! To make matters even more challenging, infrastructure demand grows and changes with unparalleled speed and frequency. We all recognize the impact that trends like mobile computing, web conferencing, and social media have had on our own usage patterns, so it's not difficult to imagine the extent of infrastructure growth and the amount of changes required to support these. Moreover, rapidly evolving business trends such as globalization, regulation, and outsourcing have a similarly significant impact on infrastructure demand, although few business decision maker have reason to recognize that in advance. It is up to infrastructure leaders to anticipate and plan for business and technology trends, so that by the time something is needed, it's always ready.

So confronting such challenges through the years, I devised strategies and techniques for innovating without the advantages of an R&D budget, customer demand, or obvious competitive necessity. These strategies and techniques, or disciplines as I call them, can be successfully applied in any environment, whether currently "cool" or not.

There's a second reason why I think IT infrastructure is a good model for other business areas and disciplines, and that's due to the impact that recent advances, such as the cloud, social media, big data, and analytics will have on business innovation going forward.

Technology is integral to every business and industry now, and will play an increasingly critical and strategic role in the future. Because of big data and analytics, the information available to companies will be far more sophisticated and powerful, allowing analyses, predictions, and insights that were never before possible. When combined with the new capabilities offered by mobile, cloud, social media, and other still-emerging trends, innovation possibilities are magnified immeasurably. They are also democratized. A wider than ever group of employees will have increasing opportunities to innovate *strategically*, creating business value and increasing competitive advantage in ways that they never could before.

I asked John Swainson, president of Dell Software and former CEO of CA Technologies, if he could discuss the nature of technological innovation as it has come to be practiced today. His response aligns completely with the point of view readers will find in the chapters that follow:

> A lot of innovation happens because of the ability to connect different technologies together and the new capabilities that they enable. It wasn't one thing that made the iPod; it was a series of advances by many people in microelectronics, micro hard drive technologies, communications technology, software, and media technology. Apple's great insight was integrating and then creating an ecosystem around all of those things. Nothing in the iPod was new. It was certainly refined—and delivered to the marketplace by Apple—in a way that was uniquely better than its predecessors. But what was really innovative was the way the system worked. And I think many of the things we call innovations in the future are going to be innovations because of the way people put different components together.

The Eight Disciplines

Then where do we go from here? How do we begin the journey to understanding and making innovation a way of life for ourselves and our organizations? This is where the eight disciplines come in. Readers may be wondering: ". . . is she really saying there are only *eight* things people need to know in order to be successful innovators?" No, unfortunately not. It's just that these eight disciplines are the ones that I've seen even the most competent, skilled, and hardworking people struggle with. These aren't the only difficulties, of course, but they're the major ones. Once we understand and put the disciplines to use, we can achieve better focus with our energy, intellect, and passion. We can better create business value and increase competitive advantage by pursuing the ideas and opportunities that propel them forward.

Also, as any Chinese person will tell you, if you must choose a number, choose eight—it's the most auspicious number we have! And it also happens to be just about the upper limit of what people can typically remember, not that there's a need to memorize these disciplines. If they apply to us, we'll know right away. However, for those of us who do have a reason to memorize them, I have leveraged a simple naming convention to make it easier. I've chosen just one word to represent each discipline, and then doubled up on the first letter so there are two Ls, two Ps, two Cs, and two Es: Listen, Lead, Position, Promote, Connect, Commit, Execute, and Evolve.

In naming and organizing these eight disciplines, of course, I needed to choose an order. It would probably be confusing, I thought, to put Listen after Commit, for example. However, these disciplines are not intended to be seen as individual elements of a linear process. Not at all. Instead, we should regard them as competencies that successful people carry with them everywhere they go. Much like the five senses, they may not all apply at any given moment in time, but each of the eight should always be on the ready every waking moment.

Here, I'll mention them each briefly. Each one is the subject of its own chapter in the pages that follow.

LISTEN. What could be easier or more routine? Well, I'm sorry to say that neither is true! Listening is difficult and surprisingly rare, but the riches we can uncover—and the difficulties we can avoid—when we learn to really listen are incalculable.

LEAD. Innovators are always leaders, by definition. However, the full set of leadership skills comes more naturally to some than to others. And there is no single skill more essential to an innovator than knowing how to lead.

POSITION. This is the how we move from where we are to where we want to be, defining an agile and competitive business model and a strategic roadmap for achieving our future vision and goals.

PROMOTE. One of the most overlooked and under-practiced disciplines that innovators must master is knowing how to create awareness, understanding, and appreciation for the value of their innovations and their brand.

CONNECT. No one innovates alone. No innovation exists in isolation. Innovators reach out across and beyond traditional boundaries to bring together the ideas, expertise, and experiences of diverse people, disciplines, solutions, and industries.

COMMIT. Successful innovators take a personal "no turning back" approach that inspires others to join in, yet also accommodates learning and change without losing sight of the common goal.

EXECUTE. Innovators know how to deliver value in the present while paving a path to the future. They find their way through experimentation and learning, and execute flawlessly. Innovators make progress and fuel progress at the same time.

EVOLVE. When innovation is business-as-usual, the search for improvement never ends. Innovators don't rest on their laurels; they barely even glance at them. Change is hard, but constant change is harder. Innovators know the drill.

Many people believe that the most common challenge facing corporate innovators is other people's "natural" resistance to change. I don't believe that at all. Sure, we will always encounter people who are stuck in the mud and unwilling to consider new and better ways of doing things. However, I think that most of the people we encounter on a daily basis just want to feel that they are part of the solution, not part of the problem. And they will usually feel—and become—one or the other based on our expectations of them. That's why our goal, as innovation leaders, is not to convince people to support our creative, new ideas. Rather, our goal is to inspire and support people in seeing, seizing, and achieving new and better ways of creating business value. And our mission is to create an environment where the word *natural* describes our approach to innovation. Each of the eight disciplines in this book provides principles and techniques to help innovators to achieve that mission, clearing the path for themselves, their teams, and their organizations.

Dean Kamen, the renowned inventor and entrepreneur, spoke to me about innovation in a way that is similar to what we did at State Street when we challenged our team to find a new way to approach our data networks. As Dean put it:

> Instead of teaching people how to go find an answer that already exists, or see how people have already done this and make an incremental change, we try to convince our people to start with a clean slate based on technologies that might not have been around when people first solved this problem. By applying a new set of technologies that weren't available in the past, they can stumble around in the dark, try these new technologies in ways that had never been done, fail a few times. But then—aha—some great new solution appears that's just fundamentally better than the class of solutions that now address this problem. And that's called an innovation.

★ ★ ★

In the chapters that follow, I give you a closer look at the essential nature of the eight disciplines. I introduce you to three different levels of effectiveness for each discipline, which you can use to assess your current and desired performance. I provide workplace-proven techniques to help you adopt the disciplines and pass them on to company teams. I discuss my own experiences using the techniques and provide a few selected case studies showing them at work. Finally, in the context of everything I've talked about previously, I provide interviews and insights from some of the world's most noted innovators and leaders.

To start, then, let's turn to *Listen*, the first of the eight disciplines of innovation and the foundation of all successful change.

聽

Chapter 1

Listen

When people ask me to describe the first step on the path to innovation, I say, "*Listen*! It's all about the Art of Listening. It's listening to learn!"

Most of us assume that we know how to listen, whether it is music playing, birds singing, or people talking, but in my view, all we're really doing is just hearing. Listening is something much deeper.

Several years ago, I saw a PBS public service announcement that opened with a composer sitting alone at his piano. We could see his frustration and despair as he struggled, without success, to craft his melody. Suddenly, his efforts were interrupted by the sound of flapping wings outside of his open window. He turned to watch as a flock of birds arranged themselves on telephone lines, as if they were notes on a bar of music. He tapped out the notes on his piano that the birds had formed and listened to the melody. Quickly, he turned that melody into an elegant symphony, and the message "be more inspired" appeared on the TV screen. To me, this is the essence of listening and the heart of innovation. When we listen to the world around us, we will often find inspiration—or even just important information—from the most unexpected sources.

Since the time we were children, our parents and our schools helped us to become better readers and better writers and better speakers. But if we think about it, how often did we have lessons in listening? The education system doesn't even recognize listening as a discipline. That's too bad, because I believe it is critical to so many things we try to accomplish in life, including innovation.

As we carry on in our careers and social lives, most of us do become accomplished *hearers*—instead of listening to exactly what someone else is trying to tell us, we're often thinking about what *we're* going to say in response. Certainly that can serve us well, but hearing and listening are as different as noise and music. If innovation is to happen in our businesses, we must become—and our team members must become—an organization of listeners.

Listen 聽 *Ting*

聽 *ting*, pronounced in a level tone and Romanized in the Pinyin system currently in use in China, belongs to a word group for "ear," represented by the pictograph 耳 *er*, at the upper left corner of the character. One listens with one's ears. On the upper right side is the character 直 *zhi*, meaning "upright," "straight," or "direct," which itself is made up of the ideograph 十 *shi* for "ten" and the pictograph 目 *mu*, rotated 90 degrees, meaning "eye/eyes." To listen includes seeing whatever is not heard. On the bottom right of 聽 *ting* is the pictograph for 心 *xin*, which represents the heart. Before the advent of anatomy and modern science, traditional Chinese culture viewed the heart as the organ for thinking as well as for feeling, demonstrating the interrelation between thought and intuition. Even today, most Chinese people would refer to the heart as the organ for thoughts as well as feelings.

In use for thousands of years, and to a great extent to the present day, 聽 *ting*, the character for the *act* of listening, implies that to listen fully one must have one's ears ready, one's eyes open, and one's mind clear, giving the speaker total, undivided attention.

Footnote: In Modern Chinese spoken in the north, on which the national tongue is based, there are 4 full tones: level, rising, dipping, and falling, as well as a half-tone or neutral tone. A pictograph refers to a Chinese character derived from Ancient Chinese Oracle bone carvings. They are visually close to an actual picture of an object. The term for the sun, 日 *ri*, was originally a circle with a dot in the middle, clearly a picture for the sun. An ideograph such as 十 *shi* for "ten" is not exactly a picture. It may be a symbol to stand for ten. Someone would have to explain to a child that 十 stands for ten.

I began learning about listening at a very young age. When I was growing up in China, parents taught their children that when adults are talking they should stay quiet, listen, and learn.

This was my father's practice as well. He always let his guests do all the talking, and he was a perfect listener remembering everything they said. I can still picture him sitting in his chair, with a slowly burning cigarette resting between his lips, and one eye slightly closed to avoid the smoke, hardly ever saying a word. Occasionally, he would ask a question.

Interestingly, my parents always put these two words together: listen and learn. They believed the best way to learn is by listening, and the Chinese character for "listen" illustrates the proper technique of listening.

Patience, Humility, Respect

It's hard to listen. Listening requires patience, humility, and respect for others.

Most of us in the business world are under a great deal of pressure. We are asked, ask ourselves, and ask others to do a great deal in very little time. As a result, we often cut others short either by ending the conversation or by shutting our ears before we fully understand what they're trying to tell us. Listening wholeheartedly requires patience.

Humility, and in particular acknowledging to ourselves that we know very little—and that often we don't even know what we don't know—also makes better listeners of us. By acknowledging the limits of our personal knowledge, we admit that we have much to learn, and so better prepare ourselves to listen to those who might teach us something.

Listening also requires respect. In fact, there is no better way to demonstrate respect for others than by paying close attention to what they have to say. By doing so, we highlight every speaker's importance and our own opportunity in being able to benefit from their knowledge and wisdom.

Successful innovators need to be in constant communication with a broad group of people from diverse backgrounds, industries, geography, and generations, including our customers, employees, senior management, colleagues, partners, and vendors—all the key stakeholders. What we learn from committed stakeholders allows us to be more responsive to changing business requirements, client expectations, and advances in technology—all within the context of our organization's unique objectives and constraints. Also, listening and learning about the market and our competitors helps us better position our company for innovation and success. It also allows us to identify and resolve potential issues early in the process.

As my father always said, "You can't *learn* while you're talking." (My mother would always nod and smile, and say, "That's right. Really smart people don't talk very much.")

We also need to listen to the younger generations. Many of us grew up in a time when we accumulated useful knowledge and informed perspective only as we aged. It is still true that many important lessons are leaned only through time and experience. However, there are so many new phenomena and experiences—social media is a great example—that only the young people among us have grown up with and truly know and understand. Different age groups can bring very different perspectives, each with unique values.

My teams always leveraged intern programs and consistently benefited from the contributions and perspectives of the young students who worked with us. For example, Anna, a recent intern, was an expert in social media. She reverse-mentored many of us and played a key role in the development and rollout of our corporate Innovation Community, one of State Street's most popular collaboration sites, with thousands of followers from all over the globe.

Listen: Levels of Effectiveness

Listening occurs at three basic levels. The more effectively we listen, the more we learn and the more productive we can be as we set out to accomplish new goals.

Level One: Selective Listening

At Level One we listen only to information that meets our immediate agenda. Often, under the guise of listening, this level can take the form of frequent interruptions and narrowly focused questions designed only to elicit answers consistent with our interests, not to enlarge our knowledge. At this level, we listen only for what we want to hear, and interpret what is said from our viewpoint alone.

Level Two: Engaged Listening

We reach Level Two when we engage in productive back-and-forth discussions, listening to the viewpoints of others and often expanding our own understanding as a result. At this level, respectful give-and-take dialogue results in acquiring knowledge and producing creative outcomes and helps build long-term relationships.

Level Three: Deep Listening

At Level Three we go beyond *what* is being said to *why* it is being said. We probe deeper, uncover individual assumptions, and seek fresh approaches and new information. We also read body language and may notice patterns that not even the speaker is aware of, which help us gain more insight into his or her true message and motivations. At this level, we are also listening to what is *not* being said.

Preparing Ourselves to Listen

To listen wisely, we must have an open mind and no agenda. We should prepare ourselves to hear something new. In fact, we should be prepared to hear *anything* that is said to us, and, at least for the moment, reject nothing.

That means having conversations to which we bring no preconceptions that could distort our understanding. It means listening to what *others* are saying, especially when what they are saying is *not* what we expected to hear, or what we wanted to hear. And it also means listening to what people are not saying.

We must also momentarily suspend disbelief and come to the conversation willing to listen to what others have to say—without judging the rightness or wrongness of it until they have had a chance to fully explain themselves. The psychologist George Miller puts it this way: "In order to understand what another person is saying, you must assume that it is true and try to find out what it could be true of." We can also think of it as an attempt to enter the speaker's reality as fully as possible, but without closing the door on your own.

Hard as it may be for some of us, we should be prepared to hear our ideas challenged if we make it clear from the start that we *want* to hear the truth.

Let's approach it another way: Listening is about creating an atmosphere of trust. That can be rare and difficult to establish in organizations. In many corporate cultures, the bearers of bad or controversial news is treated as if they were to blame. It is common to hear managers say, "Don't come to me with a problem, come to me with a solution." After hearing that, how many employees do you think will bring up issues that need to be addressed? Too often it can lead people to hide problems they can't solve on their own, instead of seeking help. It's important that team members have the freedom to find solutions without having to bring the problems to management first. However, they must also feel comfortable escalating problems that they don't know how to solve. Leaders who keep listening will know the difference, offering support where it's needed, and inspiring others to act without fear.

Sam Palmisano, the highly regarded and recently retired chairman of IBM, knows the importance of listening. Sam had been at IBM for a long time, joining the company in 1973. After a successful start in sales, he caught the attention of upper level management, and he rose rapidly through the company's ranks. He became president of the company in 2000, CEO in 2002, and chairman in 2003. You would think that an accomplished executive who had been around IBM for so many years would know everything there was to know about the company. Sam didn't think so. As he told me,

> It was no accident that the major work effort I launched at my first senior leadership meeting as IBM chairman was a collective online "jam" on who we are and why we exist. It included tens of thousands of employees re-examining the company's core values. Some of it was contentious and brought up feelings not typically aired in corporate forums. But the result was a credible definition of values, shaped and endorsed by IBMers themselves.

As I will discuss further in the next chapter, I was fortunate enough to have had Sam Palmisano as a mentor while he was president of our business unit at IBM.

How I Go about Listening

When I arrived at State Street in 2001, I made the usual rounds, introducing myself to the company's upper level management and the heads of all the major business units. I wanted to listen to what each of them had to say about service quality. I also wanted to listen to any other issues that touched on technology infrastructure. Finally, I wanted to listen to their business challenges. I came out of these meetings with a strong sense of the needs and issues that these executives wanted to see addressed. One, in particular, rose to the very top of my to-do list. It was a vendor pricing issue mentioned by Ron Logue, who then headed up our biggest business unit. I had been quite surprised when he brought it up, since IT vendor issues don't typically require the attention of the company's business executives. I could tell from the tone of Ron's voice and the expression on his face, though, that this bothered him greatly. I knew that if I could solve this problem for him, I would gain his trust and confidence in my ability to solve the rest as well.

First, I did my homework, collecting data and facts. I spoke to everyone who had anything to do with this contract and vendor. I got copies of the old contract and the new one, and sat down to read each one in detail. I could hardly believe it when I saw that the old contract had terms and conditions that gave the vendor clear rights to increase the price up to double the amount of the current payment. Evidently, the details of the pricing agreement had either been missed or lost in the five years since the contract was signed. The vendor had done nothing wrong—other than not "listening" well to an unhappy client. I knew their CEO and sent him a note. I explained that I had just joined State Street and I was looking forward to working with him again. He left me a voice mail saying, "Madge, congratulations! If there is anything I can do to help you to be successful there, please let me know!"

I assembled a team of IT, procurement, and finance people to start working on the new contract. Our team met with the vendor team many times to try to come to a mutual understanding. Over the years, however, a great deal of hostility had been built up, and the team made little progress at first. I called their CEO to take him up on his offer and to let him know that I could help him be successful at State Street, too. Together, in partnership, we found a much more reasonable starting point. Seeing the results of our collaboration energized the team. They worked, in partnership, to improve the contract terms even more. However, the business executives, still feeling stung by the unexpected increase, remained reluctant to enter into a new commitment with a vendor they had come to distrust. I called their CEO once more. After a long talk, he agreed to a total reduction of more than 70 percent from their original proposal. This single to-do item, which resulted in annual budgeted expense savings of millions of dollars, let Ron Logue know that I had listened to him. In addition, it reestablished a sense of partnership with an important strategic vendor whose product was an essential component of State Street's application platform at that time.

What does this have to do with innovation? Everything! Great ideas cannot succeed on merit alone. They can succeed only when they are built upon a strong foundation. As innovators, listening allows us to understand and align our efforts to the objectives of our business leaders. It helps us uncover the root causes of issues and envision feasible solutions. And it forms the basis of our partnership with the people and companies on whom our success will depend.

Here's an example of listening as practiced by Tom Mendoza, vice chairman of NetApp, the global data storage company. He was able to nurture enough trust among employees that they were willing to tell him the truth—some bad news about how hard it was to make improvements in the company's processes.

> I want people who want to work here. I want them to be honest and open. I want them to feel safe. I want them to be positive. I want leaders who lead. And I want to embrace change. So I ask specific questions everywhere I go: "How do you think we are doing? What can we do better?" We had a particular location where the performance was good, the numbers were good, but innovation was being stifled. People had candor and courage, and they trusted me enough to tell me what was going on. It blindsided me. It blindsided everybody else. And, oh by the way, they were right. The lesson I learned was that you can't assume that things are good just because in general they feel really good. There could be certain areas where you really are stifled and you don't even know it.

"Listening" to the Facts

As we listen to others, we should keep an eye on the facts as well— facts and data as well as analytics. Listening to the facts can help us get to the root cause of the issues raised and the requests made by key stakeholders. In the same way the data might provide us additional information beyond what we heard, it can also reveal issues buried long ago by the need to develop simple procedures to get through the day or put out the fire. Finally, if most of those to whom we listen are reluctant to give us bad news—in spite of our efforts to develop trust—the data can fill that void. And while the conversations will most likely give a faithful sketch of the situation, hard data and first-hand experience will fill in the big picture. For example, when I ran IT infrastructure, I would walk the floors of the computer operations center whenever I could. I especially liked to show up when the shifts were changing, because that way I could listen to the details of what had happened on the first shift and to what the next shift planned to do about it. I also asked to receive every "incident alert" that went out, which was a unique request from a senior executive, since the normal practice is that only critical alerts are automatically sent to senior executives.

We can think of listening to people and listening to the data as two sides of the same coin. Flipping the coin again and again will help us understand the deeper realities and root causes of what we hear.

The following story by Deborah Ancona, professor of management and director of the MIT Leadership Center, perfectly illustrates the point that you have to both listen to people and look at the facts to arrive at a clear understanding. And you have to suspend your assumptions while looking at the facts, in the same way that you have to suspend your assumptions while listening to people.

> The first step in sensemaking [that is, taking different perspectives and collaboratively developing shared awareness and understanding] is what we call "letting go of your existing mental model" . . . that is, creating a new map of reality or of the ecosystem in which you're operating . . . not only what's going on inside your firm, but also the different things going on outside of your firm.
>
> This requires going out and collecting a lot of data from people who have very different points of view, so that you get a better sense of what's going on, not by checking a single pulse, but a number of them. I tell lots of stories about this,

but one of my favorite examples concerns a big oil and gas company looking to improve its revenue from one area of China.

The first thing they did was try to make sense of the current situation: Why were they losing market share? Looking around, they saw the other global players were all losing market share, too. How could that be possible? The team was told to go back and dig into the data again. They looked and they dug, but the data still showed that they and their competitors were all losing market share. Typically, when we get disconfirming data to what we "know" to be correct, we often just look harder to find the answer we want, instead of the truth. And that was what they were doing.

Finally, they gave up looking for confirming data and went back to talk to their people on the ground in China. They were told that their competition was local: they were being eaten alive by small Chinese operators. The team had never even thought to look at local operators, because their mental model had them competing only with other top global players in oil and gas.

Local operators had never before been able to compete because they didn't have economic resources to do so. But as things had changed in China they got access to more resources and now were popping up all over the place. So part one of sensemaking is knowing how to look beyond what you ordinarily look for to see what's really happening.

Once they had done that, and had identified the local operators, they could move ahead, but in a very different way. Their solution? They started partnering with these local operators and in that way were able to regain a pretty big chunk of that market.

For us sensemaking is a quintessential part of leadership. But it's also a quintessential part of large-scale innovation. If you are going to innovate, you need to see the world differently to understand what's going on out there. And you need to bring together diverse mindsets and different inputs to brainstorm different ways of thinking and operating.

What Deborah is discussing is the concept of *disconfirming data*: information that is inconsistent with our beliefs and expectations. Modern psychology has actually coined the term *confirmation bias* to describe the human tendency to focus on information that confirms what we already believe and to simply ignore information, or disconfirming data, that does not. Great listeners and curious minds share a keen interest in disconfirming data, knowing that it often signals an opportunity to learn something new, or to understand a very different perspective on what we already believe to be true.

Listening to What Is *Not* Being Said

Another important characteristic of great listeners is that they go beyond the words. They watch body language, they notice patterns, they make a concerted effort to understand the reasoning and thinking behind the words they are hearing. John Swainson, president of Dell Software and former CEO of CA Technologies, told me how careful listening combined with additional facts and knowledge can bring us to a totally new understanding. In addition to his other achievements, John was at one time general manager of the Application Integration Middleware Division, a business he founded for IBM. In this example, he describes the origin of IBM's Websphere product, a software solution that revolutionized and simplified web application development.

> Very often, people will tell you what their requirements are, but they understand the requirements only in the context of today's products and today's technology. They can only tell you what they know. For example, before Websphere, people kept telling us they needed ways of attaching legacy applications to the Internet world. What they really needed—but couldn't articulate—was a new way of writing a new class of applications, particularly e-commerce and transactional applications. They needed to be first-class players on the Internet with a web-facing programming model and yet be able to access legacy data sources. Through a process of experimentation, listening, and learning, we came to understand what the market

requirements really were. In summary, we were able to use our understanding of where the technology was going, combined with an understanding of the real customer requirements and a bit of intuition to understand how customer economics were changing.

You have the advantage of a deeper level of insight into what the technology enables to be possible. And, because you get to talk to a lot of customers, you hear the problem described from a lot of different levels of maturity and points of view. If you do this properly, you have a unique opportunity to start thinking about what the fundamental problem really is that we are trying to solve, as opposed to whatever the last customer I talked with said. You have to figure out what the inhibitors to their business being more successful are and what technology now makes possible.

The example that John discusses here very effectively demonstrates the essential role that listening plays in successful innovation and the multiple steps that it requires. First, John listened to his customers in keeping with the principle of "assuming that what we're hearing is true and trying to find out what it could be true of." This led him to go beyond simply listening to *what* they were asking for, so that he could also understand *why* they were asking. That helped him gain a deeper understanding of the essential problem that they were facing. Next, John looked at the facts—the number of customers asking for similar assistance. And then, he combined what he heard with what he knew, which led to the development of an entirely new solution.

In a similar vein, here is Nathan Myhrvold, who we heard from in the opening pages of the book. Like John Swainson, he discusses the need to "step outside and beyond the immediate" to understand the larger issues—and larger opportunities—involved.

It's wonderful to listen to your customers when they have suggestions to improve your product, that's a great thing to do, but much of that is not very innovative. Because—guess what—your competitors are listening to their customers as well. Plus, although the customers have a very important point of view, it's not the customer's job to know what's technologically possible. The car was not invented because people complained to the folks in the stable who took care of horses and said "Hey, I would really like to have this thing so that it doesn't involve a horse." That isn't how it works. So you have to be able to step outside and beyond the immediate.

I met Dr. Tenley Albright, now Director of the MIT Collaborative Initiatives, when she served on State Street's Board of Directors. Tenley has a fascinating personal history. She spent most of her career as a surgeon. Before attending Harvard Medical School, however, she earned worldwide recognition as the first female U.S. figure skater to win both a world championship and an Olympic gold medal. She tells a wonderful story about listening beyond the words as she practiced for one of her world-class performances:

I was at Davos for the world figure skating championship and was practicing my routine in an outdoor rink. A judge—I remember he had white wavy hair—was watching me. When I paused after a new move I had been practicing, he came over and said, "You're not going to put that in your routine, are you?"

I was surprised that he would ask me that, and I had to think about it for a moment before I answered him. What went through my head first was that he must not like what I'm doing. Otherwise, why would he say that? Then I thought . . . well, he probably hasn't seen anything like this before. I like to make things up, do something different, try new ways to skate familiar elements. So I decided I wouldn't take his remark as an insult.

I answered him very politely, "Yes, I am."

I *did* listen to him, and I did *think* about what he had to say. But I decided not to take the move out of my program. It was important for me to be open-minded about his comment, but I had to stick to my inner belief. And of course this was when I went on and won the world figure skating championship for the first time.

The lesson for me was you always have to listen. What people are saying may bring out issues you need to consider. But if you are going to innovate, you have to expect that not everybody will like or accept what you are doing. Plus, you have to go with what you might call your "gut" or your intuition. I don't think you can innovate if you shut out your intuition.

As Tenley's wonderful story demonstrates, good listening doesn't require us to discard our intuition or accept another's viewpoint without question. However, it does require that we momentarily set our beliefs and convictions aside, in order to understand someone else's.

Tenley has another story that can teach us something more about listening to what is *not being said*. It is listening for, and questioning, underlying assumptions. Tenley was a pre-med student at Radcliffe at the height of her competitive skating career. After becoming the first American female skater to win Olympic gold, she was ready to move on to her next challenge, becoming a surgeon. However, she still had a full year of undergraduate study to go. Or so it seemed.

And I thought, I wonder if you have to graduate from college in order to go to medical school? So I went to see a neurosurgeon at Children's Hospital who was a mentor of mine and I asked if he knew the answer. He didn't, but he checked with the administrative offices in Chicago, and got back to me. He said, you know, it's a written requirement that you need premedical courses, but nowhere can we find it written down that you have to graduate from college. So as a result I applied to Harvard Medical School. I had about seven interviews there, and I think they were skeptical at first. They must have thought competitive skating was a bit like fan dancing! But they finally admitted me. I must admit that partway through medical school I realized I could have used a little more of the other courses, but I made out fine, and I had some absolutely wonderful professors. So, I think innovation happens when you're able to be open-minded and are willing to ask questions and quietly challenge assumptions.

Before we leave this chapter on listening, I'd like to return to the source of my ideas on the subject—my family in China—and tell a story of a miraculous episode of listening that changed my life:

After finishing college, my father went out to sea, rising through the ranks in oceanic shipping, and becoming a captain. For many years, he could be found at the helm of large cargo ships plying the Pacific Rim. (He later became the master of other captains, and he spent the peak of his career managing both business and staff for one of the largest shipping companies in Hong Kong.)

For several years, my parents traveled between Shanghai and Hong Kong, still a colony of Great Britain. They finally settled down in Hong Kong with my brother, while my three sisters and I remained in Shanghai with some domestic help and our Grandma, who was a physician practicing Chinese medicine.

One spring, I wrote a very important letter to our parents. I suggested that the four of us—Margo, Marjorie, Marsha, and me—leave Shanghai and join my parents for a summer vacation. That spring, Mother was accompanying Father on his freighter sailing in the Indian Ocean. Normally, we always sent letters addressed to Mother. This time, however—most significantly—I addressed my letter to Father. I asked that we be allowed to visit them during our summer vacation and see some of the lands they frequented in those days—India, Hong Kong, Singapore, Burma (Myanmar), Ceylon (Sri Lanka), and Japan.

Father listened and understood. By addressing the letter directly to him, rather than to Mother, he thought I was requesting his personal assistance. As my younger brother, Michael, recalled to me later, as soon as Mother read my letter to Father, he exclaimed: "Ayah! Nai-Ying, the girls want to get out!"

Father immediately wrote a letter inviting us to visit them on his ship, and my sisters and I took his letter to our local police station and applied for a "temporary" exit permit allowing us to spend a summer vacation with our parents in Hong Kong.

Our request was approved, and we were authorized to visit Hong Kong for the summer. We packed a single suitcase with enough clothing for all of us, and left behind everything else we owned, including Mother's jewelry, calligraphy, paintings, everything.

We embarked on our summer vacation and settled down in Hong Kong with the rest of the family. Farther had understood from my letter that it was time for us to leave Shanghai for good and rejoin the family. This was a desire on my part that I really didn't understand myself—really an unconscious desire at that time. But Father had listened beyond the words, and he understood!

Listen—Concrete Steps for Putting This Discipline into Action

How then, can we create an organization that truly listens—that, in effect, puts its ear to the ground to discern what's really going on, as the company in Deborah Ancona's story eventually learned to do?

Individual

First and foremost, we ourselves must change our own behavior and become listeners rather than hearers. Listening, unlike hearing, is not a natural act, and we must learn to listen and choose to listen. I'm always surprised by the reaction I get from people when I talk about this. They get it. They usually grasp the idea immediately and seem genuinely interested in honing their listening skills—especially when they see that by listening, they will discover opportunities and benefit from the insights of others. One of the best ways to develop better listening skills is to pay special attention to our reaction to disconfirming data—information that is at odds with what we think or believe. The usual response is to ignore or dismiss it. Sometimes we argue against it. When we're listening, we actively pursue it with curiosity, humility, and respect.

Team and Organization

To get a team listening, team leaders can suggest practices like "listening to the voice of the customer," designed to gather input regularly, and then to act on it. They can also be encouraged to implement regular information-sharing processes that keep them in touch with changes happening inside and outside of the organization. Most importantly of all, in every team, there are those who do most of the talking and those who do very little. Team leaders can make a special effort to ensure that every member of the team weighs in with their thoughts on important topics and to monitor the ensuing discussion closely to help encourage thoughtful and respectful listening.

At the organizational level, executive leaders must themselves demonstrate this type of advanced listening—just as, for example, Tom Mendoza has. They should take care to appoint people with open minds and good listening skills charged with creating an environment that encourages people to communicate honestly and openly. They can work to identify and break down barriers to listening—between individuals, teams, divisions, management, customers, and partners.

How to Listen
- ✓ Show respect for the speaker—maintain eye contact
- ✓ Clear and open your mind and heart to listen—give the speaker your full attention
- ✓ Do not have preconceived expectations regarding what you are about to hear
- ✓ Don't judge as the speaker speaks, but question when you don't understand
- ✓ Never assume what the speaker will say—ask questions to clarify before making assumptions
- ✓ Make sure you understand exactly what every word means
- ✓ Never interpret until the entire message is heard
- ✓ Look for new information in the conversation
- ✓ Make the discussion about the speaker's beliefs, not yours
- ✓ Control your body language—do not cross arms, or signal boredom or a closed mind
- ✓ Preserve your facial expression—with a little smile for encouragement; do not express disappointment or impatience on your face

✓ Notice the speaker's body language. Look for clues as to *why* he or she is telling you this, not just what

✓ Reflect on what you were told. Look for the root cause and validate with other data

✓ Look at any data you have to see how it compares to what you've been told

領

Chapter 2

Lead

Throughout the decades of my management career, many top executives and managers helped me grow professionally and become more street-smart. Some of my toughest managers made me stronger and more resilient. IBM excelled in training its managers, and I was the beneficiary of that training. None of it, however, could compare with the effect that Sam Palmisano, the now-retired chairman of IBM, had on my developement as a manager. I was lucky to be the recipient of his personal advice, and I was able to observe him in action. I have to say he became the most important leadership role model of my career.

When Sam became the president of the IBM subsidiary I was working in, he immediately invited ten of the company's female and minority managers to join his diversity council. I was assigned to work on the mentoring program, and so had the opportunity to be mentored personally by Sam.

Sam did not fit the stereotype of top executives in those days. They tended to be straitlaced, very serious, impersonal, reluctant to engage in social conversation, and not much fun. He was different and better in every way.

When it came to getting things done, Sam "drove" me and everyone else along the high-speed lane, with a laser focus on our business results. That's not unusual for any successful leader. But there was more to him—a rewarding personal side that was unusual in an executive at his level. I saw him operate and engage his people with humility, openness, honesty, optimism, warmth, a lot of laughter, and fun. He even used humor and personal storytelling in his interactions with employees. Everything he said and did—the *way* he said and did—even the expressions on his face had a profound impact on me. I learned from Sam how important and powerful this personal connection can be. It motivates and inspires people and can bring them together to achieve a common cause. It helps them perform beyond their own expectations and reach achievements they never knew were possible. Encouraging people to have fun in a hard-driving environment is part of the leadership equation I learned from Sam, and it became part of my own style. Why not have some fun along the way? It keeps everyone's sprits up and makes the long hours and hard work much easier to accept. People are more creative, productive, and bonded, more willing to help each other and collaborate, when they are having fun.

Leadership is essential in any endeavor, and even more so when it comes to innovation. Each of the industry leaders I interviewed while writing this book, including Sam, spoke at length about the role of leadership in terms of innovation. There were many common threads and no apparent areas of disagreement among them. They certainly echoed my own convictions, and they did so with great clarity and precision. Because of this, I have made a special effort in this chapter to use their words to share these important insights about what it means to lead innovation.

> **Lead 領 *Ling***
> 領 *ling*, rising tone, means "to lead." Ling can also mean "the collar of a robe," long considered the most important part of a garment. On the left side of the character is the

ideograph 令 *ling*, which stands for "decree or order," supplying both the sound of the character 領, as well as implying that a leader may also be guided or commanded by a decree or a mission, an order or a command, or a directive. On the right-hand side of the character 領 *ling* is the character 頁 *ye*, which stands for "page/pages," implying that orders, decrees, missions, and tasks were often written down for clarity, and a leader can fulfill his/her mission best if it is stated clearly in writing.

Just as there are many styles of successful leadership, *ling*, when combined with other words, can be used to express many different ways of leading. When 带 *dai* is placed before 領 *ling* to form the term 带領 *dailing*, the combination in modern Chinese means "to bring someone along into territory/territories with which one is already familiar but the one brought is not." The one brought may be a child or a novice, depending on the context. The modern Chinese term 領導 *lingdao* means "to lead by instructing, guiding, or showing the way in simple steps."

Note: Sometimes a part of a Chinese character may indicate its pronunciation. It is not so in every single instance, nor does that indicator always work, because over thousands of years the characters may no longer sound the same. Sometimes the pronunciation reference still works in one of the Southern Chinese dialects, which may be closer to ancient or traditional Chinese than pinyin, which transcribes the pronunciation of the newer dialect spoken in Beijing, China.

Ancient China refers to pre-Confucian times. Confucius lived and taught from 551–479 BCE. Traditional or Imperial China refers to the period between the Unification of China in 221 BCE to the end of imperial rule in China in 1911.

Note: page/pages. Singular or plural is not normally distinctive unless the number is to be stressed. In general, how many of anything is less important than the thing itself. Here, whenever a Chinese noun is used, as in page/pages, a slash is used to indicate that linguistic difference between English and Chinese.

Leadership Essentials

Often, when people think of *Leadership*, they think in terms of executives or managers. In an innovation culture, however, a leader is anyone who takes a stand to bring about new ideas that add value to the business and the organization. We don't need to be a top executive or a manager to speak up and offer ideas and concerns in an effective, fact-based way. We don't need to directly supervise others to inspire and recruit them in creating value for the company and customers. Anyone, in any role, can lead by example—mentoring and growing the next generation and giving the young opportunities and support.

Dr. Eugene Y. Chan, the physician, innovator, and entrepreneur who founded the DNA Medicine Institute, is a great example of a young person who did not let his youth or status as a student hold him back:

> The Human Genome Project was underway when I was a student at Harvard Medical School, and I remember wondering what would happen afterward, how would people access genetic information? I think just asking that question changed everything for me, because I started thinking about the world, and myself, a little bit differently. It evolved into a very clear focus: What exactly is going to happen to the field of genome analysis and how can I be a part of it?
>
> As a young person going through the system, doing your homework and studying, you learn about all the great discoveries and movements in science and you think it's all so much bigger than you. But just daring to think you can actually change it was the first step for me. And so, once I was on that track, I focused on how to create a technology to access genetic information a lot faster. And that led to the creation of U.S. Genomics, which raised $120 million, has commercialized three products, and has partnerships with all sorts of companies and people.
>
> It's leadership of ideas. I think that starts with staying true to a question that really means something to you and then

being fearless in going about your process and what you're pursuing.

Eugene's description of his own development as a leader perfectly depicts what I consider to be a fundamental aspect of leadership: It's not about having staff or responsibility or power. It's passion.

Leading with Passion

Ming Tsai is a celebrated chef, entrepreneur, cookbook author, and host of his own TV cooking show. Ming's famous restaurant, Blue Ginger, is five minutes from my house in Wellesley, Massachusetts. We first met Ming just after we moved to Wellesley and went to the restaurant to celebrate my daughter Michele's birthday. Ming came to our table to say hello, and he charmed us all. His food was so delicious that Blue Ginger became our family's favorite restaurant.

He speaks from experience about the need for passion in our chosen vocations.

> You have to follow your passion in life. At school, I graduated with a mechanical engineering degree from Yale. My dad is literally a famous rocket scientist so—as any good Chinese boy would—I figured I should be a doctor, lawyer, or engineer, and I took the engineer route. In my junior year, I told my parents that I would finish my degree, but I really didn't want to be an engineer. I wanted to be a chef. I wasn't sure how they'd react to that. Well, my mom gave me a big hug. She told me how lucky I am that I know what I want to do at such a young age. She said, "Give it your all. We support you 100%." My dad accepted it too, telling me, very bluntly, that I was not going to be a very good engineer anyway! He was right, and I know that because I didn't love it. If you don't love what you do, if you're not passionate about it, you will never be good. You'll just go through the motions. And I think that's true in any industry. If you love what you do, things just come so much more easily to you.

Tarkan Maner, previous CEO of Wyse Technology, serial entre-preneur, and investor, is one of the most passionate leaders I know. He is also a wonderfully warm and positive person. Conversations with Tarkan are often brief lessons in history and philosophy and are always inspiring, funny, and thought-provoking. How many Turkish-born executives have an American "favorite founding father," I wonder? Tarkan does.

> Benjamin Franklin was so right when he said that human beings can be categorized into three types. First are those who are immovable. We all know them. Second are those who are movable, and we know them as well. Third, and this is my favorite category, are those who just move. And I think that not only do they just move, but they also keep moving, and they move others along with them. A leader not only does the work, but also inspires others to do the work for a great cause. A great leader moves those who are movable, and inspires those who are immovable.

Tarkan's reference to a "great cause" leads to another essential element of Leadership—vision. It is a vision for the future that's able to ignite the passion of others and unite them as a team.

Leading with Vision

Think about some of the words used to describe great innovators: visionary, inspirational, evangelist, revolutionary. They're terms that describe a contagious passion, a viral enthusiasm that can move through an organization like fresh air through open windows. John Swainson, president of Dell Software, and former president and CEO of CA Technologies, calls this a sense of shared purpose and shared adventure, which I have always found comes from having a compelling vision of the future.

> You can't guarantee innovation, but you can remove the constraints and create the conditions for innovation. People

sometimes think that they can get innovation by creating an innovation program and giving speeches about innovation and putting a suggestion box in the corner. In my experience, that doesn't work and actually creates cynicism. Innovation is not something that happens because you tell people to go innovate. It's something that happens when you create an environment that encourages it, when you reinforce that with the right economic and social signals, when you have the right people in place, and when those people have a sense of shared purpose and shared adventure.

Shared purpose, shared adventure—they focus people on the impact of their efforts, the "why" not just the "what" of their job. When a results-focused vision and passionate shared purpose exist across an organization, it engages people, makes them think about ways to improve, and causes them to view change as natural and expected. It creates a sense of urgency that drives collaboration and progress.

Admiral Michael Mullen, former Chairman of the Joint Chiefs of Staff under both Presidents Obama and Bush, provides an example of the ultimate shared purpose—saving lives:

> We created a command in the Pentagon called the Joint Improvised Explosive Device Defeat Organization (JIEDDO) because we were losing so many lives to IEDs, improvised explosive devices. Congress quickly funded roughly a billion dollars to this office whose single focus was to figure out a way to get ahead of the enemies with respect to IEDs. And this focus on saving lives immediately broke down a lot of barriers. This guy could do things that no one else could do. He was able to get directly connected to those in Iraq and Afghanistan who were in the fight. He created a feedback mechanism for resolution of technical difficulties, which normally takes weeks or months, but he could do it in a matter of hours. He created an analytics group that allowed much more rapid analysis in terms of what the problem was and what a possible solution was. Even though they were located in Washington, it was as if they were fighting on the ground.

They had a huge impact in terms of getting ahead of the IED problem. It was a lot of money and it was a lot of leadership cover—and we were losing a lot of lives. So there was a great sense of urgency. When you're losing lives, there is nothing more serious.

Few of us, of course, get to spend our workdays coming up with ways to save lives. However, innovation leaders do frame their vision with similar clarity and urgency that inspires.

John Thompson, CEO, Virtual Instruments and former CEO, Symantec, attests to this important fact of leadership life:

> Leaders have to inspire their teams. If you can outline something that seems compelling enough, exciting enough, and doable with significant benefits, then they are all ready to buy in. They know that if the company does well, so do they. That's clearly what happened at Symantec, when we made the declaration that we were going to be the leader in securing the web experience. Everyone in the world recognized that was a big, big issue and someone had to step up.

Passionate leaders invest themselves and their organizations in inspiring causes that are aligned with their organizational mission. As Tarkan Maner explains:

> San Jose is in Silicon Valley, the capital of technology innovation. Yet I found out that half of the students in San Jose didn't have computer access to the Internet. I thought, if that's what it's like here, imagine what it's like in towns and cities that aren't high-tech. Imagine what it's like in countries and villages that aren't even developed! So this is my passion, to make sure that every student in every school across the globe has their own connection to the Internet and can learn to their fullest capacity.

With this vision in mind, Tarkan's team developed a low-cost, no-maintenance device that does not even require a power cord, allowing more schools to offer their students educational access to the internet.

We might think that saving lives, securing the web experience, and educating the world's children are somewhat beyond our reach, at least now. Perhaps. But we can still have a results-focused vision and shared purpose that creates value for our company and instills passion in our people. Ming leads by example here:

> The best part of being a chef is creating something new and knowing that because of that new dish or that new service, we can actually make people happy. *And that is what drives me.*
>
> Your goal should not be that you want to be successful. Success is not a goal. Your goal should be how can you serve, how can you make the biggest impact with your skill set, do the most for that business to create something and help others. Every night I go home and I know we've pleased a lot of people. People leave happy. They may come in grumpy, but they leave full and satisfied. They may come in sad but they leave happy. You can really affect someone in a two-hour time-frame. And it's not rocket science! It's not like what I studied in college! It really is very basic: creative food that's a good value, excellent service, and respect.

Respect, Trust, and Integrity

And with that point, Ming leads me to another set of essential attributes of leadership: respect, trust, and integrity. They are inseparable.

Sam Palmisano speaks once again about the online "jam" he discussed in Chapter 1:

> Those values that our people shaped have held up remarkably well as a distillation of what it means to be "an IBMer." We still have a long way to go to make them real in everything we do, in our management systems and our behavior. But I think it's safe to say, after nearly a decade, that we laid

the right foundation. And I am convinced that the transformation we have carried out since then was only possible because we first undertook this deeper dive of self-discovery—because we not only made "trust and personal responsibility" one of our values, but we demonstrated it in how we created them.

Respect, trust, integrity. These qualities are essential to success to every person at every level of the organization and in every facet of life. However, leaders have a special responsibility as role models. Their actions, good and bad, are magnified.

Leadership is Tom Mendoza's passion, and respect, trust, and integrity are his not-so-secret weapons of choice. I recently congratulated him after *Fortune* magazine, for the second year in a row, named his company, NetApp, one of the top ten companies in the world to work for. Tom was thrilled, telling me that NetApp is actually in the top ten in fifteen different countries. In fact, he explained, in the last five years, only five companies on Earth their size or larger had met with greater success. Tom says he no longer has to convince people that what his company is doing actually works. He just explains the essence of it. And I've never heard anyone articulate the importance of respect, trust, and integrity the way that Tom does.

When someone says "people are our most important asset," I say, "Tell me how you demonstrate it. And take money out of the equation. Don't tell me how much you pay somebody. Tell me what you do to show them." I believe that if people know that you genuinely respect and care about them, that you have their interests at heart, they will follow you anywhere. What I think all great leaders have in common, across any culture, across any industry, is that people come through for them. Not because they are afraid. Not because they are intimidated. They just don't want to let their leader down. If your people feel appreciated and respected, they are not going to leave at five o'clock figuring somebody else has the problem. They are going to help you innovate to solve it.

The Soft Skills of Leadership

Ming agrees, and extends our discussion to the soft skills of leadership, where emotional intelligence is required. These soft skills are what allow us to connect with others through empathy and understanding. It's how we create relationships built on respect, trust, and integrity. It's how we enlist the help and ingenuity of others in reaching our goals. It allows us to dissolve obstacles rather than fight them.

> Leadership requires soft skills because the way you treat your people is exactly how they are going to treat your customers. Never forget that, because if you treat your people with arrogance or attitude, they are going to treat your customers like that. You have to treat everyone with respect. As my dad says all the time, the people who work for you and look up you are the ones who will help you rise to the top. They are also the ones that can protect you from falling to the bottom if something goes wrong. If you don't respect them, they won't respect you. And if people don't respect you, then they don't want to join your journey. My dad makes people feel like they're in charge. I mean, he's always been the boss, but to his subordinates, they're the ones making the decision. And I learned from that.

Ming told me a great story about the way his father taught him to acquire soft skills. When Ming was only five or six years old, his father would have him return purchased but unused items to shopkeepers. In addition to giving him this great responsibility, Ming's father would add a challenge. He would not give Ming the receipt. He would just send the young boy into the hardware store, for example, with pliers or a battery and no receipt. It was up to Ming to speak to the shopkeeper in a way that earned a full refund. "I'd tell them it's not the right size. . . . I am sorry, but we found the right one and now we need our money back." Ming explains. "I wasn't rude, I wasn't forceful. I was respectful and told the truth and I always got the refund."

I have great admiration for the way Ming's father taught him how to deal so effectively with others. It breaks my heart when I see how many decent, talented, hardworking people lack this critical skill. I believe that having emotional intelligence often differentiates those who succeed from those who just work hard. It differentiates great leaders from high performers. High performers can accomplish many things, but great leaders can accomplish even more because they inspire and align others.

Once again, Tom Mendoza beautifully captures the spirit of emotional intelligence in action. He provides a profound leadership example of understanding what his people need in terms of support—and when they need it:

> Many times, leaders offer inspiration *most* when it is needed least, and offer it *least* when it is needed most. When people call after you've had a big win, by the fourth or fifth call, you are not inspired. I've called salespeople when they miss their goals and said "Hey, I understand you had a tough year, don't worry about it. We have your back. You have been great for many years, don't look backward, look forward, we have your back." I tell people, when you have someone's back, don't keep it a secret. Things like that make people feel like they want to go to work. They work hard and when they get that call, that's the call they never forget. They all forget the fifteenth call after the big win, but they never forget who was with them when it wasn't so obvious. We want our people to know that we understand their challenges. We know we're asking for something difficult. Going at the rate we go is hard, we get that. We make sure they know we appreciate it, we understand the struggle.

Leaders who combine emotional intelligence with a high standard of excellence inspire people to be their best.

Gerald Chertavian is the founder and CEO of Year Up, the program that helps low-income youth prepare for success in school and professional life through education, training, and internships. He explains:

Generally, there is a bigotry of low expectations for inner-city residents. However, we have high expectations, and we combine them with a lot of support. We don't see those as being mutually exclusive. You support the heck out of someone, but you never lower the bar. In a lot of environments, there's a willingness to accept less than the best, or to lower expectations—somehow born out of a stereotype that our young people aren't capable, smart, or able to deliver at very high levels. We fundamentally know that's not true, so we challenge people significantly on a daily basis. It's possible to be deeply supportive and still have a system in place that holds people accountable. And our students want that. Many young people say—no one ever thought enough of me to hold me accountable. No one ever thought enough of me to extract the best from me. We do. I don't think the motivations of human beings differ based on race or economic status or ZIP code.

Under the right leadership, seemingly ordinary people can do extraordinary things. Here's a brief story I first heard in a training class at IBM that brings the point home.

One sunny day, a boat full of people made its way up a fast-moving river. All of a sudden someone yelled that a child had fallen into the water. The passengers started screaming for someone to help, and amidst the confusion they saw a man plunge into the water. After an anxious moment, he reappeared on the surface of the water with the child in his arms. Once the man and the child were back on the boat, everyone began to applaud. Someone asked the man, "Where did you get the courage to do that?" The man responded with his own question: "Who pushed me?" Great leaders know how and when to push others to achieve more than they themselves thought they were capable of achieving.

Before we leave this topic, I'd like to return for a moment to Admiral Mullen. Despite having held one of the most powerful military positions on earth and overseeing more than 2 million people, the admiral is a very modest man. During our interview, he was very generous with his time and his thoughts on innovation, and you will see many of his comments throughout this book. However, I must admit that one of my favorite insights into the admiral's leadership philosophy came not from him, but from an online comment *about* him. It was just one of many about the admiral's integrity and the trust and respect he inspired among his troops that appeared after an interview in the *Harvard Business Review* (http://hbr.org/2012/06/admiral-mike-mullen/ar/1) was published online.

A young man who had served under Admiral Mullen wrote in about the time he was charged with an alcohol infraction—his third. He expected to be separated from the Navy with an "other than honorable" discharge. Instead, Admiral Mullen gave him the opportunity to attend a Navy alcohol rehabilitation program that would allow him to continue his career. The young sailor did so, and Admiral Mullen even attended his commencement when he finished the program. The sailor recovered, graduated, then rose through the ranks and completed a 22-year career in the Navy.

I found this humanitarian story particularly touching and insightful, and it is very representative of the role that an exceptional leader often plays in the lives of others.

Sound Judgment

In addition to demonstrating his compassion, this story also illustrates Admiral Mullen's sound judgment as a leader. The capacity for sound judgment is another critical success factor for leadership, and I believe instinct also plays a part in the way those leadership judgments are formed. In any decision, many human factors are always involved. A leader's instinct and judgment both will have a major impact on the organization's future and on team members' lives.

John Thompson explains, "Leaders get paid to be instinctive, not to be rote and routine. The most successful leaders are the ones that have an ability to anticipate market changes, anticipate changes in customer needs, and anticipate the issues that are troubling their employees. That's what leaders do. These are not necessarily instincts you're born with, but you need develop them over time as you gather experiences and learning."

Great leaders have a sense of tomorrow. We have too many people in executive positions in companies who only focus on today's numbers and not what might be happening the next day. Great leaders and innovators who use their instincts as well can guide their teams through remarkable innovative work in their industries.

Creating a Culture of Innovation

We have covered many topics so far: speaking up with confidence; following our passion; having a vision and inspiring others; demonstrating respect, integrity, and trust; emotional intelligence; high expectations; judgment. Yet, believe it or not, these are just the basics. I think that all leaders, whatever their role, need these qualities to succeed. Those who succeed at leading innovation must do even more. They must also create a culture where innovation can thrive.

Culture is an organization's collective assumptions, norms, and values. It defines what is—and what is not—acceptable behavior, using both positive and negative reinforcement. Leaders hold the keys to creating a culture that values and supports innovation. And the most important key for unlocking the ingenuity of our people is the one that changes how we think about and manage failure.

Nathan Myhrvold, the inventor and former chief technology officer at Microsoft, expresses some key insights into the nature of Silicon Valley innovative culture:

One attribute of the Silicon Valley culture that's really important is that if you are part of a start-up and that start-up fails, it doesn't mean that people won't hire you. In fact, they are very apt to hire you. Things fail for lots of reasons. Just because it fails doesn't mean it was a bad idea or the people in it were bad. Maybe a few of the ideas were bad, maybe a few of the people were even bad, but by and large, failure is a kind of tuition. It's a very expensive tuition, and frankly, you would rather have somebody learn about what doesn't work on someone else's dollar. So it's been the culture in Silicon Valley for the last 30 years, that hey, if your start-up doesn't work out, that's okay. Silicon Valley is very forgiving. If it wasn't that forgiving, then it would be very hard to maintain the pace of innovation. When I travel in Europe or in Asia, people there will sometimes say, "How come we don't have a Silicon Valley?" And I ask, "If one of your startups raised $50 million, hired a whole pile of people, went high flying and then went bankrupt, would you hire those people?" And many of them say, "Well no, of course not." So then I say, "That's why you don't have a Silicon Valley!" Because if you create a culture where everyone has to play it safe at all times, they won't take the risks necessary to do something new. A lot of companies want to be innovative, but then they don't do anything to create the right incentives for their employees to take risks. I'm not saying that failure is the goal, but failure has to be okay.

Nathan likes to use baseball as a way to make this critical point because the rules of that particular game reward hits more than they punish strikeouts. He explains:

Let's say you have a .330 batting average. Well, that means that 70 percent of the time, you strike out. How terrible! But you would actually be one of the best hitters in baseball! So the coach doesn't say, "You failure! You should be hitting 100 percent of the balls!" No, they tell you, "That's great—you have a .330 batting average!" Well, innovation is even riskier than hitting in baseball. So you need a culture where it's okay for people to strike out sometimes. If you expect innovation to be really easy and always positive and always wonderful, then you have the wrong expectation. And you're ultimately not going to succeed in it, because as soon as the going gets tough, you're going to get timid.

Inventor Dean Kamen attacks the subject with equal passion and conviction:

Most big companies—most organizations—are about avoiding failure. Just think of the word *management* itself. A company that's well managed has very predictable results; they control the environment and avoid surprises, because typically surprises are bad. So management is about not having unpredictable outcomes, while innovation *is* an unpredictable outcome! I think this mind-set is why many organizations unintentionally define success as a lack of failure. I don't. I think success is doing something better than anybody else has ever seen or reported it being done. And if it's that good and that valuable, it's called an innovation.

Dean is careful not to imply that failure never has a downside. He's saying that the downside can and should be managed. We just need to get past our fear of failure in order to do so.

I think big organizations need to assertively take some amount of their resources that they can responsibly put at risk, some amount of their people that they can responsibly allow to do things that will probably fail, and say, "Go do something different. If it fails, we can deal with that, we can take that pain. If it succeeds, we will increase the rate at which the world gets better solutions to its problems." I think if big organizations deployed their resources that way, you would see the rate of progress accelerate rather dramatically, because big organizations have lots of resources; they have a lot of smart people. Dean talks about failing "responsibly," which means recognizing the difference between failures that can put an organization or its customers at risk, and failures that are part of the path to success.

It would be irresponsible to bet the farm and have people destroyed or companies destroyed. But taking small risks, knowing that you are probably going to fail a bunch of times, but that you can afford the emotional and financial risk of doing so, is one way that a whole organization can end up being more innovative than other organizations who are steeped in the belief that failure is bad. It's possible to create an environment that encourages people to try to innovate by giving them some sense that failure—when done responsibly— we can tolerate it. It's part of life and failure can be of a project and not of the person. And as long as you can limit

the downside of the failure in terms of its impact on an organization and on your resources, it's okay.

In the past, especially in large organizations, this critical distinction
was rarely made. Any failure jeopardized reputations, careers, and jobs.
As a result, people naturally avoided risk. When failure happened
anyway, rather than learn and then share what they had learned with
others, people often felt the need to minimize the failure, even cover
it up. This mind-set is still deeply embedded in most large organizations today, and reinforced in ways that are not just limited to things
like promotions or pay. Those who fail are often made to feel alienated
and outcast. Contrast that with the culture that Dean has cultivated at
DEKA:

> What I do at DEKA is let people know that it's okay to apply
> different technologies or different thoughts to conventional
> problems and see whether they lead to unconventional but
> better solutions to those problems. Most of the time, they
> don't. But people can work on a project and have a result be
> a failure without the person being a failure. And people see
> an environment that doesn't punish individual failures, as long
> you learn from it and move on. We actually celebrate our
> failures; we make fun of them in a positive way. We call it
> frog-kissing. You know, you can kiss a lot of frogs and get
> nothing but warts, but every once in a while, you kiss a frog
> and it becomes a prince or a princess. At DEKA, particularly
> for people that have come here with some experience in big
> companies, it takes them a little while to recognize what's
> going on. When I ask them to do very difficult things, I per-
> fectly understand they are going to try and they are going to
> fail. We are not going to punish that failure; instead, we are
> going to recognize the time and the effort and the energy
> expended as well as the disappointments. We support people
> who try things, and we won't punish them. After a while,
> people start getting excited about doing things in ways that
> have never been done before. And, as they do, they keep
> finding all the ugly reasons it wasn't done that way—it doesn't

work, it was too expensive, too this, too that. . . . But every once in a while the intersection of new good ideas and new and better technologies allows somebody to walk into my office and say: "Hey, look at this, it's smaller, it's lighter, it's faster, it's cheaper, it's more reliable. It's a better solution to an old problem." Then we celebrate it and, often, it creates enough value that we now have more resources to try other innovations. It can be expensive up front, but if you believe in it, and you have a little bit of courage and you are willing to fail, it works.

As you might expect, Tom Mendoza's company does not equate success with a lack of failure.

Companies can be innovation-crushing machines. They group-think, and they try to eliminate risk, which basically eliminates innovation. When we crafted our value statement, we said we will take risks. I often tell people, "If you don't take a risk, you just took a risk. If you don't make a decision, then you just made a decision. There is no safety in not doing something. There is no safety in just thinking *if I sit here, I won't get hurt.* Innovation needs a culture that says that if we are going to innovate, we are going to risk, and that means that some things are going to work and some aren't. So let's go. . . .

To move forward, leaders must introduce and maintain a failure-tolerant culture. This requires that they dig deep into the organization to ferret out practices that encourage the old mind-set and replace them with approaches that support managed risk-taking and leverage the learning from failure in the interest of innovation.

Even in a culture that supports fast failure, control is still possible and still necessary. Jim Phalen, executive vice president and head of operations and technology at State Street Corporation says,

Our business is heavily regulated, and rightfully so, given the amount of assets we hold and the systemic risk for the markets as a whole. Innovation in this environment means more costs and more controls. You can't experiment in ways that lead to headlines in the papers and huge losses for your shareholders. But regulation doesn't mean sacrificing innovative capability. It's not an excuse or a barrier. In fact, regulation is an advantage, if you see it in terms of specialization and service. So we have a huge opportunity to be innovative in our markets. For example, State Street created the first ETF. I remember sitting at the management committee meetings when we were evaluating the concept along with a few other product development opportunities. The asset management team had envisioned a product similar to our passive product, but with real-time valuation and real-time market processing, and it would trade like a stock rather than a fund. The good news is that we funded the ETF effort. The bad news, in hindsight, is that we didn't bet the ranch on it! We made a few other bets at the time too. But, when you're primarily selling risk products, you have to think about protecting the downside.

Calculated risks seek the optimal risk/reward trade-off in a way consistent with clear organizational guidelines and practices. These guidelines specify the "tolerable limits" of downside exposure (e.g., investment, resource time, reputation, client impact, etc.) and structure innovation initiatives in a way that allows them, if necessary, to fail early and with minimal investment. "Failures" within these limits are clearly learning experiences. To make those failures yield some value, however, leaders must also ensure that the lessons are actually learned and shared with others, so they won't be endlessly repeated.

Obviously, leadership is a complex, multifaceted, and critically important topic. Admiral Mullen tells us:

From a leader's standpoint, I think you have to do a pretty thorough and honest self-evaluation and figure out if you are capable of leading innovatively. If you are not, then I think you need to hire individuals who are, and you need to delegate to them, empower them, and support them. They need to be properly incentivized individually for outcomes, and the organization needs to be properly incentivized if you are going to produce innovative ideas.

The three levels of leadership effectiveness below can assist us in performing the type of self-evaluation that the admiral recommends.

First, however, I'd like to share a story from Dr. Eugene Chan. It provides us with two powerful reminders about leadership. The first reminder is that leadership does not always come naturally. The second is that the most innovative leaders of all are those who can lead and change themselves.

When I started my first company, I had never managed anyone ever in my life. Even running just a small staff of people quickly turned into a disaster. It's one thing to be book smart and get A's on your tests, but having soft skills and dealing well with people was a completely different skill set that I'd never even thought about. So I had a lot to learn in that regard.

The lowest point came when half my company quit on me. I was maybe two years into it, and I clearly didn't know what I was doing. I think we had maybe ten or twenty people at that point and there were multiple things going wrong. I hadn't budgeted correctly, and we were running out of money. Communication with my staff was incredibly poor because, at that point, I thought it was all about me, not my team members. Basically all these things came to a disastrous outcome when half the company quit, and I had rebuild it.

So I went into a period of self-reflection, and I had some external consultants come in and help me out. It took me about a year and a half before I saw the light, and then things became much more effective. The difference was like night and day.

Part of it is learning to be responsible, learning how to take care of your team members, and trusting that your team is the most valuable thing that you have. Another part is being a good communicator, so people don't have to guess what you are thinking. You have to articulate exactly where things are going—not just the big vision, but also the concrete little stuff that gets you there. Because when you do, you can actually see your powers amplified. In addition to having ideas and technological skills and know how, now you've also got all these amazing people with you on your team helping create something that's pretty incredible.

Lead: Levels of Effectiveness

Now, let's look once again at the different levels of leaders' effectiveness for this discipline and give ourselves the opportunity to locate ourselves and determine whether we need to make improvements in our performance.

Level One: Limits Ingenuity

At Level One we are limiting ingenuity, often acting as the "brain" and treating others as arms and legs that are there strictly to execute instructions. We are incapable of inspiring others with a clear vision or allowing others to feel a sense of ownership. Leaders at this level are unable to gain the trust and respect of others. Solutions are implemented in a way that generates a "compliance mentality" and fails to bring about desired change. We are unaware of the ways in which the business's existing incentives encourage people to remain tied to the status quo.

Level Two: Leverages Ingenuity

At Level Two we are doing much better, leveraging ingenuity, communicating a clear and achievable short-term vision, and creating enthusiasm, ownership, and accountability. We are able to gain the trust and respect of others through demonstrated integrity. We involve others in designing and implementing solutions, increasing buy-in and reducing resistance. There is a focus on enhancing or supplementing incentives (e.g., compensation) to support accountability, initiative, and teamwork and to minimize penalties for limited risk-taking and failure.

Level Three: Cultivates Ingenuity

At Level Three we are at the top of our game, cultivating ingenuity, upholding a compelling future vision and a strong sense of shared purpose. We always inspire others to do and be their best. We align incentives, social cues, and processes to encourage and manage creativity and change. Emotionally intelligent and highly regarded, this leader challenges and supports others in achieving beyond their own expectations, and actively supports processes that enable experimentation, constructive failure, and learning.

In many organizations, the passion and ingenuity of employees go untapped. Leaders at every level have the opportunity to harness incredibly abundant yet often underutilized resources. Such efforts will not be wasted. As Admiral Mullen told me, "People get a tremendous amount of personal satisfaction with a job well done, with the opportunity to create, to give back, to make a difference. You need to cultivate that. If innovative people do not have a leader to connect to, they are going to go somewhere else."

Lead—Concrete Steps for Putting This Discipline into Action

Individual

Leaders exist at every level of the organization, not just in the management and executive ranks. John Quincy Adams, the sixth president of the United States, said it best: "If your actions inspire others to dream more, learn more, do more, and become more, you are a leader." Leaders articulate a clear vision and invite others to share their passion. They set high expectations and support others in achieving them. Leaders build trust, respect, and integrity by demonstrating it. They work hard to develop emotional intelligence and sound judgment, learning from every experience and emulating the leaders they most admire.

Team and Organization

Innovative cultures encourage experimentation and learning. They do that by ensuring that their expectations, processes, and incentives are all closely aligned. Clear guidelines for acceptable risks are communicated to employees, and people who do the right thing the right way are not punished when they don't get the "right" results. In fact, they're rewarded for their willingness to advance progress. Processes exist to ensure that the organization as a whole is able to learn and benefit from their experience.

How to Lead

✓ Possess a passion to lead and a will to win!

✓ Show integrity, energy, urgency, positivity, self-confidence, trustworthiness, and compassion.

✓ Define an innovative vision—a sense of tomorrow

✓ Create a culture for innovation—lead by example, encourage, inspire, and reward innovation

✓ Initiate changes; take calculated risks fearlessly

✓ Communicate effectively with all stakeholders inside and outside the organization—knowing what to say to whom, how, and when

✓ Exercise sound judgment and emotional intelligence—understand the proper timing for saying and doing everything

✓ Bring a positive attitude to solving challenges. There's always a way; if not, we build the way

✓ Earn respect; don't rely on compulsion or an official title

✓ Strive to make a difference—focus on your legacy and create enduring strategic value

計

Chapter 3

Position

When I ran global IT infrastructure functions, I would often say to my staff, "By the time the business asks us for something, it's already too late." What I had in mind is that it's unrealistic to expect business leaders to consider or even recognize the extent to which their strategies and initiatives will rely on infrastructure. When they're strategizing new global business models, for instance, nobody at the table is talking about network connectivity, response time, or security architecture. Nor should they be. Yet these essential services must be in place to support the execution of that business strategy. Infrastructure leaders can't wait to be told what the requirements are; we need to anticipate and prepare for them. And that requires us to understand the direction of the business, match it to advances in technology, and create a roadmap that is agile and flexible to support the business growth.

A Roadmap for Change

All innovation leaders need roadmaps that allow them to achieve their goals and realize their vision. Roadmaps are strategies that plot our course from where we are to where we want to be.

My leader and mentor, Sam Palmisano, told me,

The core responsibility of leadership is to understand when it's time to change—the organization and yourself—and what not to change, what must endure. Getting those right is hard—especially today, since so much is changing, and at such velocity, and in such unpredictable ways. Whether you lead a business or a government, there is tremendous pressure to deliver short-term results and quick fixes. To thrive in such an environment, it's important to manage for the long term. At IBM, we've thought about this a lot—about what enables an enterprise or institution to survive and thrive through decades, much less a century.

What I find most encouraging is that the forward-thinking leaders we work with around the world are not just achieving measurable success in the short term; they are innovating in ways that will create virtuous cycles for a generation or more. They are building systems.

One of the ways that innovation leaders manage this is by leveraging the discipline that I call *Position*, the subject of this chapter. Positioning is the process by which we identify where we want to be, how we plan to get there, and what milestones and deliverables we will achieve along the way. Positioning also includes trying to anticipate and responding to the twists and turns we will encounter along the path. Positioning can be thought of as a game of chess. When we first learn to play the game, our focus is very immediate. We scan the board to identify pieces in immediate jeopardy, protecting our own or capturing our opponent's. The object of the game, of course, is to capture our opponent's king. We don't get points for capturing other pieces; however, we hope to weaken our opponent's position and draw closer to striking distance of the king. As we gain skills and experience, we can think a few steps ahead. We intentionally target valuable pieces and set up a series of moves to achieve our goal. However, we're still just inching forward. Our eye is on the king, but our plan is many steps behind. Finally, as we become more advanced players, the focus shifts. Now we can play the game in accordance with a master plan. We still develop and execute interim strategies, but they are part of a deliberate and orchestrated effort to achieve our ultimate goal—capturing the opponent's king. That orchestrated strategy is our roadmap.

As in chess, where the position of the pieces change throughout the game, our roadmap won't be much use if it assumes the environment around us will stay static as we proceed. Effective positioning requires us to anticipate how the future will unfold and to develop our roadmap accordingly. In some cases, we can recognize changes that are already underway, forecast what will happen with fairly good certainty, and draw our roadmap to account for them. In other cases, we might be able to anticipate likely scenarios, yet not know which of these will actually come to pass. That requires us to develop our roadmap in such a way that it can respond quickly and effectively to each of those likely scenarios. Of course, there are always cases where we will be confronted with the completely unpredictable and unexpected. Our roadmap must be developed with those in mind as well. We do that by staying as agile and flexible as possible, avoiding backing ourselves into a corner with unnecessary assumptions.

Position 計 *Ji*

計 *ji*, falling tone, belongs to the radical or root group 言 *yen*, for words or speech, which is itself comprised on the left of the ideograph for transgression over the pictograph 口 *kou* for "mouth." On the right is the ideograph 十 *shi* for "ten," which the Chinese consider a perfect number, representing fullness. 計 can mean "to strategize, to scheme, to calculate, to calibrate, to seek a plan, to arrange," or "to evolve a plan." Leaders, worldwide, have multiple plans. Many times stakes are high, and when Plan A is in progress, a resourceful leader would have Plans B and C ready in case Plan A encounters an obstacle which may delay it or too time-consuming to overcome, or the factor may have shifted, so that Plans B and C could be immediately implemented. There were many legendary Chinese leaders who possessed this ability in their leadership.

Positioning is certainly more of an art than a science, and one that we get better and better at with experience. We can also learn a great deal from the experiences of others. Many of the innovators I interviewed for this book had quite intriguing stories to recount.

Positioning Our Sights

As we discussed in the prior chapter, having a vision for the future is an essential attribute of great leaders and innovators, as there is no roadmap without a clear vision of the future. In this section, we look at several examples of innovative business positioning.

John Thompson, CEO of Virtual Instruments, has a natural ability to position effectively. I asked him to talk to me about his time as CEO of Symantec, and have included the transcript of his answer as follows:

> Symantec was originally created through the consolidation of two small PC tool companies. The strategy that had evolved during the PC era was all about the yellow boxes dominating the shelves of retail stores around the world. And, sure enough, if you were to go into a Staples or Best Buy, you'd be overwhelmed by a sea of yellow boxes. And the company did very well, going from essentially nothing to $632 million in 1999.
>
> But then the Internet revolution arrived and the market was giving far more value to true Internet companies than to more traditional software companies. It became clear to board members that the company did not have "an Internet strategy," since despite $632 million in revenue, the company had a market cap of only $1.3 billion. By contrast, many of the Internet companies of that era that had gone public barely had any revenues, yet had multiple billions of dollars of market cap. So it was clear that our strategy was not appealing enough to investors to the point where they were willing to invest in the company. And that's what prompted the board make the change in the leadership.

I arrived in April of 1999 after 27 years and nine months at IBM. And I remember, as I was considering the job, I called this friend of mine whose board I served on to ask his opinion on whether I should take on the role of chairman as well as president & CEO. His advice to me was, "You're going to have to do all the work, anyway so you might as well have all the titles." But then he also said, "You know it's important for you to think about what you are going to do when you get there. But don't preordain the answer now. Take time, listen to the team. Don't be bashful about sharing your opinion, but use your ears and mouth proportionately. Listen more than you talk for at least the first 100 days."

And that's what I did. I focused first on understanding why the company was doing what it was doing and why we weren't doing some of the things that other more market-successful companies were. So, by the time those first 100 days were over, I'd settled on the strategy, which was to become the leader in securing the web. During my first analyst meeting as CEO, I said we were going to refocus our company on securing the Internet and becoming a leader in that space. We had a very prominent position with Norton Antivirus, and we would put far more energy and effort around security than anything else. I also indicated that, to the extent we could, we would get out of those businesses that weren't relevant or important to securing the Internet. And we did.

And so the first business that we got out of was the ACT! business, which was a personal contact management database. It was the best in the market, but it had missed the CRM space and so there was no reason for us to hold on to it. We sold that back to the original founders and then embarked on trying to sell Visual Café. That was also a market leading tool, but not relevant to what we were trying to do, and quite frankly, other than the distribution strategy that Symantec had, it had no relevance to anything else in the portfolio.

We did keep PC Tools, because it had a very, very strong revenue base. The growth was not overwhelming, but it was highly profitable and we felt we could use the proceeds from that to invest in the security business. There was no clear leader in the security business at that point in time. Many people would say that McAfee was a leader in the corporate space and that we were the leader in the consumer space, at least around antivirus. But there was no clear security leader because the security category was evolving as the Internet evolved. So, the end result was that we picked our strategy after listening and put a stake in the ground that publically said we intended to become a leader in the security space. Within one year of making that declaration, we changed our nomenclature to becoming the leader, which was yet another signal to the marketplace that we were going to be more and more aggressive.

Soon after the announcement, we bought a little company in Virginia called URLabs that had a relatively new, early piece of technology around URL filtering. Back in those days, large corporate users were concerned that the Internet was going to become a distraction to their employees and it could create liabilities for them. And so they needed to filter more of the places that people would go on the web, particularly if they were using corporate assets. So we thought that this would be a good step for us, moving more toward the corporate market, not just the consumer space. And it would fit within the cash budget that we had. We executed one or two other small deals and then we did the big deal, AXENT Technologies, which had very, very strong leadership in enterprise security management. And that was, yet again, a very, very, clear signal to the marketplace that we were targeting not just the consumer franchise that we had, but the enterprise as well. And we were targeting it in a way that was very, very meaningful, because we spent $600+ million for AXENT, which was probably 30 to 35 percent of the market cap of the company at that point in time.

Not long after, in 2001, the Nimda attack occurred. In under half an hour, it became the most widespread Internet virus in history, and our business just exploded. We split the stock three times over the next three years. The market cap of the company I think peaked at roughly $25 billion, up from that $1.3 billion when I joined. So we were feeling pretty good about ourselves. I had only planned to be there five years, and I was ready to retire. But then we decided that the world was changing. Because of the web, more data was being produced every day than companies could effectively secure and manage. And the nature of the threats was evolving in such a way that if you couldn't block the attack, you could at least recover the information. The market leader in backup and recovery then was Veritas, which had gone through a pretty difficult time with a number of market misses, and the stock had been hammered pretty badly. And so our vision evolved to the point where we thought we should be in the security and information management business, not just the security business.

And that led to the acquisition of Veritas, one of the biggest deals ever announced and executed in the tech space. I will say it was the toughest deal that I ever did in my time at Symantec. It didn't turn out quite like I had hoped for the company. But we were committed to continue to evolve our business and meet what we thought were the changing needs of the marketplace, which were not just to secure the content people were creating, but to evolve our business to keep up with customer needs.

John's story is filled with fascinating insights into how he repositioned Symantec and developed and executed a roadmap to achieve his goal. Notice, too, that he spent a great deal of time *listening*, the subject of Chapter 1, when he first arrived at the company. Later in our conversation, John went on to explain why he invested in and now leads Virtual Instruments, again positioning himself and his company for the future:

I think infrastructure performance management is going to become the critical issue, now that we have virtualized everything in the IT space. My belief is that at every inflection point in this industry's history, a new problem emerges that people have never thought about. And with each new problem, new leaders evolve. When the world became client/server enabled, distributed systems management became a huge, huge issue. Solutions like Tivoli and CA and HP OpenView all evolved, and that's now a $15 billion business annually. When the world became web-enabled, security became a big issue. Antivirus technology existed before web enablement, but it was the advent of the web that really, really catapulted that business to the forefront and expanded what people's definition of security was. And I think now as we move to a more *virtualized or cloud-based environment*, there is another likely shift. The old systems management tools were architected twenty years ago. And so it's more likely that a new company will emerge to focus on something that is unique to the new environment.

This market shift that John describes was echoed in comments made by State Street Executive Vice President Jim Phalen, when he spoke about the fact that what was once a relatively small Boston bank, around for hundreds of years, is now one of the most systemically important financial institutions in the world.

We had a major turning point in the 1970s when we moved from being a traditional commercial bank to becoming a custody bank and asset manager. At the time, State Street was the fourth of the big commercial banks in Boston, behind Bank of Boston, Shawmut, and Bank of New England. It was a very bold decision at the time to take a nontraditional path and become an investment services organization. But State Street thought the industry had a big future, and it did with mutual funds, then master trust and the pension market developing quickly. So this bold decision put us on an entirely different path. Back then, nobody would have anticipated that State Street would be the only one of those four organizations remaining as an independent firm, much less be recognized as one of the world's most systemically important banking organizations. So we made a transition from a traditional bank to a custody bank and then we became more of a global organization, and then we became an information organization as opposed to just a transaction kind of organization. Now we are moving to the point where what we deliver is a fully automated service, where technology isn't simply the tool anymore, it's the *product*.

Developing Our Roadmap

When I joined State Street in 2001, the business areas were in the midst of dramatic change, including global expansion and the move toward information delivery that Jim Phalen described. The technology infrastructure, however, had not changed in years.

In fact, since infrastructure managers had been told to minimize spending, many of our technology assets were quite old and past the end of their expected life cycle. As a result, the infrastructure staff spent most of their time trying to keep everything up and running instead of implementing new technologies. Also, a highly decentralized organizational structure left teams without a clear sense of ultimate accountability and ownership. This sometimes created barriers and resentment. When problems arose, people often felt they had to protect their own interests and find others at fault, rather than simply fix the problem.

After my first round of interviews inside State Street, I knew we needed a major infrastructure renovation. The existing platform and service model were barely meeting today's business needs. I was certain that they would not support globalization, business process transformation, or any of the other business strategies that were in the works.

I assembled my management team. After a number of meetings, our vision for the company's future technology infrastructure services took shape, and we drew up our strategic plan. We had several goals. First and foremost, we wanted a high-performing, resilient, and agile global IT infrastructure. Second, we wanted to deliver the highest quality service, something we called "global seamless service delivery." Third, we wanted to operate with optimal efficiency and cost-effectiveness, providing quality service at the lowest reasonable price. And finally, we wanted to stay abreast of emerging technologies in order to improve performance, reliability, productivity, and cost-effectiveness.

As is the case with any business undertaking, one of the earliest decisions we had to make was determining how to fund it. We employed several strategies. A major component of the strategy was an Efficiency program that identified opportunities to reduce expenses so that we could reinvest some of the resulting savings in projects that would advance our plan. We did not reinvest everything. In fact, as the next chapter on *Promote* explains, we wanted to ensure that the business areas could see the results of our hard work. So, every year we gave back budgeted expense savings to the organization, often totaling in the tens of millions of dollars annually. However, through activities such as consolidation, contract renegotiation, and many more, we knew we could self-fund a considerable number of initiatives. We also decided to leverage the technology asset Life Cycle Management, an approach to renewing capital assets without increasing expenses that I explain in the next chapter. And we developed an approach called Global Strategy, Local Execution, in which we would meet short-term needs in local offices in a way that would drive progress toward our longer-term global vision.

Once our objective, goals, and funding strategy were clear, we immediately began putting the various programs into place. At the core was a Business and Financial Management program that brought a data-driven business value perspective to everything we did, with consistency across all functions and locations. This included many elements: a metrics program, cost transparency, business and communications processes, training and templates for business case development, vendor and asset management practices, and other techniques designed to bring solid and consistent business management practices into everyday infrastructure operations.

The second program, Technology Management, addressed our strategy for advancing the infrastructure itself. It had two major components. The first was a Technology Infrastructure Blueprint that defined our three-year technology strategy for every IT infrastructure function. We outlined our common objectives, such as performance, security, continuous availability, virtualization, agility, green computing, and more. Then each of my functional teams—network, server, storage, end-user computing, security, operations, and middleware—developed individual plans to achieve these goals. These were submitted to an integration team and then presented to an IT leadership committee that included all of our major IT partners. We also created an Innovation Lab for testing new technologies and innovative products so that our Blueprint could stay constantly up-to-date. The second major component of our Technology Management program was our Global Data Center Strategy. This strategy outlined a multiyear effort to consolidate and eliminate local server rooms and implement state-of-the-art enterprise and regional data centers. These new data centers would offer the state-of-the-art security, resiliency, regulatory compliance, green standards, and other critical capabilities that we knew would become increasingly necessary for global competitiveness.

We also initiated a third program, People Management, which initially focused on integrating historically distinct functional areas into a single core infrastructure team. As we advanced, our organizational model changed as well, and this program soon became known as Global Virtual Teams. When organizations have highly decentralized and disparate infrastructure environments, as State Street had, local teams have very different processes and tools. To bring consistency across all locations, we formed a Global Virtual Team for each major infrastructure function that united functional staff across the globe. These teams worked together to implement the programs and initiatives described earlier, leveraging the approach of Global Strategy, Local Execution. They also focused on implementing global process management standards and practices, including ITIL (information technology infrastructure library) and Lean, that could quickly create consistency and improve effectiveness and efficiency. Since we recognized that creating a global culture would require a different mind-set in many respects, we also implemented incentive programs, awards, and training to speed progress.

Together, these three major programs formed the multiyear roadmap that led to the design and implementation of our award-winning 21st Century Technology Infrastructure. This solution has seamlessly supported State Street's unprecedented business growth, acquisition, and transformation while also establishing an early foundation for State

Street's move to cloud computing, real-time data warehousing and analytics. Innovators in every industry and role can develop a roadmap for themselves, their teams, or their organizations, plotting the course from where they are now to where they want to be.

Gerald Chertavian, founder and CEO of Year Up, provides another example. The whole mission of Year Up is to position young urban men and women for success. In addition, he has implemented a unique roadmap for aligning his organization to the needs of his customers.

> We're structured so that we'll actually go bankrupt if we don't adequately prepare our students to be successful at the companies they are placed in during their internship. We are tightly aligned with the sponsor—the companies—who contribute more than 50 percent of every dollar we raise to have access to the talent. This structure is not typical for nonprofits, which have traditionally been set up so the funder is a third party, such as the government, and the client is unrelated to the funder. This structure can result in misaligned economic incentives and potentially harm efficiency and quality. At Year Up, we have a self-regulating mechanism—if we don't perform well, we go out of business in six months. Because of this economic incentive, we must quickly recalibrate, learn, innovate, and change in order to stay relevant and hold ourselves accountable to providing a high-quality program.

Positioning for Change

Dr. Eugene Chan, founder of DNA Medicine Institute and several other startup companies, knows how to position himself and his work for the future of medicine and health care, just as our Technology Blueprint did for our business and technology goals. Here he provides another great example of the principles and the application of position:

> I am focused on making changes to the future course of medicine. It's a matter of identifying a key need and asking a bold

question: "How can we do this better?" I try to look maybe five years down the road to answer that question. I don't look much further than that because I want tangible things to tackle. So I ask, "What's the world going to be like in five years, and what can we do to address this need in that time span?"

One night I was doing my rounds in the hospital around three o'clock in the morning and thinking how antiquated and slow the process is from when blood is drawn to the time the physician actually gets the diagnostics. And I thought, "Hey wouldn't it be great if I had a little device in my pocket that took the place of this huge hospital laboratory the size of two basketball courts?" And as I thought about it some more, I realized there's no reason that consumers shouldn't have access to this type of information too, if it helps them take better care of themselves. People can buy a glucometer to check their own blood glucose, or get a machine that tells them their cholesterol. But these are all discrete pieces of information. As a physician, you've got a different diagnostic power in your hands when you get 20 or 30 lab values back. That's why when you're not feeling well, your doctor tells you to come into the office or go to the emergency room—it's so they can get access to all that information. Right now, we depend on this centuries-old patient-doctor interaction for testing, but many of these visits can be avoided if the person runs the test themselves and the software provides an intelligent diagnosis. Also, people who are proactive about their healthcare are going to use this diagnostic information to take better care of themselves. They can measure their blood and watch cholesterol go up and down on a daily basis rather than annually, for example. Technology like this empowers people and lowers costs. This is what I'm focused on now.

Another great example of positioning for change is the concept of business continuity planning. This ensures that companies are prepared to maintain critical operations in the event of any unexpected situation that may interrupt normal business processes. Possible threats span a very wide range, including natural disasters and weather-related situations, widespread influenza outbreaks, political or social unrest, and more.

State Street's business continuity management strategy won several industry awards for its innovative end-to-end planning model. Since work can flow across multiple business areas, functions, systems, and locations, true business continuity requires the comprehensive identification of all dependencies between and across each of these elements. This focus on workflow dependencies is incorporated into every component of State Street's program, enabling the timely identification, support, and resolution of any incident with a potential business impact, including market-, counterparty-, technology-, facilities-, and personnel-related events. This approach positions State Street to manage any incident with potential business impact, regardless of its reach, locale, or nature.

All of us, as well, need to make sure we are positioned to be ready and to be as effective as we possibly can. Here, then, are the levels of effectiveness for the *Position* discipline. I invite readers to read and recognize themselves in one of these levels, and, if necessary, use the takeaways in this chapter to help move up to the next level.

Position: Levels of Effectiveness

Level One: Reactive

At Level One we have little sense of where we are and where we want to be. It's all about firefighting rather than planning for the future. We are frequently blindsided by change.

Level Two: Responsive

At Level Two we have a vision for the future and a plan for achieving it. We actively seek information on what's around the bend, and we respond quickly to change.

Level Three: Strategic

At Level Three we anticipate trends and prepare ourselves and our teams in advance. We develop a global, integrated roadmap to achieve our company's long-term vision. We are good at achieving the long-term vision by way of executing short-term steps that bring immediate benefit to the organization.

Personal Positioning

Just as we must constantly strive to position our organization for success, innovative employees can position their careers as well. I didn't really understand the American corporate culture when I started my career. I had no idea about how much work each of us was supposed to deliver to be considered a good worker. So I always worked extra hours but never recorded any overtime, even though I knew that we could be paid for extra hours of work. I thought management might surmise that I worked extra hours because I was incompetent.

As a result, I always delivered my results before the scheduled target date and with measurable high quality. Little did I realize at the time that I was positioning myself for advancement. Sure enough, opportunity arose, and I was assigned as a project manager very early in my career.

Whenever my managers had offered me a management position, I always declined because I loved my own technical work. I personally excelled by consistently delivering high-quality work well ahead of schedule. So, my performance record still allowed me to remain highly qualified for future advancement.

However, one lucky year, when I was six months pregnant with my daughter, I accepted my first managerial position as information systems manager for IBM Stockholder Relations in New York City. So, in a single year, we were able to celebrate two blessed events.

Thereafter, for the next decade or so, IBM included me in their Executive Resource Program and I was able to move through a broad range of assignments in technology. One Friday, my manager asked me to have lunch with him in the IBM cafeteria. We each bought a sandwich and sat down in a quiet place to eat. I had barely picked up my sandwich when he told me that I was being offered a job as the site information systems and telecommunications manager for IBM in Boulder, Colorado. This was a major promotion, and everything I had done at IBM made me ready for the assignment. They planned to make the announcement the following Tuesday, and I would have to fly out in three days!

The opportunity was very attractive. My responsibilities involved overseeing all IT functions for six IBM divisions located at the Boulder site at that time and were fundamentally equivalent to those of the CIO (Chief Information Officer). Yet, my mind was racing a thousand miles a minute about the perspective personal issues this move would create. However, I also realized that this unexpected reassignment was potentially pivotal to my future career—the ultimate positioning. It could provide an excellent foundation for any executive job, especially as a future CIO.

As confident as I was to accept the challenge, my 13-year-old daughter, Michele, brought up her own issues. She was in the eighth grade, and she had friends in Scarsdale, New York, where we lived, that she didn't want to leave behind. My husband, Werner was also concerned. He had an excellent job, and he was the only child of his elderly parents, who both had serious health issues, so he could not move. We made a family decision: I would move to Boulder by myself, and they would stay in Scarsdale.

The job was a challenging, risky assignment, but it worked out and was a success. The personal sacrifice was significant, as I missed my family, but I flew home as often as I could to be with my husband and daughter.

As hard as it was, my Boulder assignment proved to be the most important job for my future career. I believe that it was the definitive experience that Merrill Lynch and State Street both looked for before offering me their technology executive jobs. I had positioned myself for opportunity with the right work experience and the right credentials. I was ready for the future.

Position—Concrete Steps for Putting This Discipline into Action

Individual

As innovators, we need to crystallize our vision for the future and develop a strategic, step-by-step roadmap for achieving it, identifying the key milestones and deliverables along the way. We need to anticipate and incorporate expected changes and be flexible enough to respond to the unexpected. Positioning applies to our careers as well. We need to strive to beat deadlines and exceed goals. We should position ourselves for the future, new opportunities, and the next advancement with the right work experience and the right credentials.

Team and Organization

Teams and organizations must manage for the long term while delivering in the short term. Leaders must clearly define and communicate their vision and strategy and by doing so provide their teams with a future goal that can drive innovation throughout the organization. The creation of strategic business value is first and foremost.

The organization and its teams must be able to focus on the future, anticipating how it will unfold and developing plans accordingly. In some cases, we can forecast what will happen with some accuracy and draw our roadmap to account for them. In other cases, we can anticipate several likely scenarios without knowing what will really happen. In still others, something completely unpredictable and even game changing can happen. Agility and flexibility are the keys.

How to Position
- ✓ Position for tomorrow, not today
- ✓ Focus on creating strategic business value—understand the company or organization's vision and goals
- ✓ Position with a strategic view from a global perspective, and fully understand every country's local requirements for defining your roadmap
- ✓ Prepare a sound business case to ensure proper decision— demonstrate financial and business benefits
- ✓ Consider all possible creative ideas, not just the current way of doing business

(continued)

✓ Exercise sound judgment in decision-making

✓ Leverage and collaborate broadly with people outside of your organization, worldwide, in different industries, and with different experience levels, to understand what might be available in the marketplace

✓ Position by focusing on your core business and leverage strategic partners with related core competencies

✓ The race is within yourself and your own organization, for continuous improvements

提

Chapter 4

Promote

In Chinese culture, we are not accustomed to promoting or talking about our accomplishments. This is not accepted as appropriate behavior. However, "Once upon a time . . ." one of my American bosses told me he was moving certain of my colleagues to the next higher level because they knew how to promote their own accomplishments. Some of them, I knew, even claimed credit for other people's accomplishments. As he put it, "Madge, do you know how to blow your own horn?" I told him that it was not in our culture to do so. He replied, "Then you need to learn American culture, if you want to work in America." I realized, hard as it was, I was going to have to learn, in spite of my culture and my upbringing. It wasn't easy, and I tried to figure out how to "blow my own horn" somewhat gracefully, so it didn't sound like bragging.

Throughout the years, as my job responsibilities grew, I came to realize that, not only did I have to make sure my boss knew about our successes, I had to make sure that he also *understood* what my team had accomplished, since we worked on highly technical issues. I came to realize the importance of recording our accomplishments promptly and accurately. I also came to see that the best way to promote achievement is through facts and data. Reporting facts and data cannot be considered bragging, so it became a very comfortable way to register our performance. I'd put together reports showing our financial achievements, how we performed against industry benchmarks, recognition, and awards. This way, my team had actual numbers to establish our financial contributions to the company—while at the same time demonstrating our accomplishments by comparison with our professional colleagues outside of our company.

Successful innovators promote our ideas and solutions across the lifecycle of our projects. In the early stages, we promote to get funding and staff. Once underway, we promote to get support and buy-in. As momentum builds, we promote to generate awareness and interest. And as we begin to realize our vision, we promote to demonstrate the value and benefits we have achieved.

Innovators can't afford to miss a single one of these steps, yet they do—surprisingly often. In many corporate cultures, innovation is seen as a type of "skunk-works" project, one that's off the traditional radar screen. There are times and circumstances when this is certainly effective, but it's not really conducive to a business-as-usual approach to innovation. And while there's often a certain comfort to operating in secret and isolation, there are costs to that as well. It's much harder to gain acceptance and integration after the fact, for example. Although many innovators go "underground" to avoid the challenges of dealing with stakeholders, there are better solutions, which we will discuss in Chapter 5, *Connect*. In this chapter, *Promote*, we recognize that more issues are caused by a lack of communication than by a surplus.

Promote 提 *Ti*

Ti belongs to the radical 手 *shou*, meaning "hand/hands," represented here with a variant used as part of a more complex character. The character itself has the root meaning "to raise, to take, to bring along or about," or "to carry." The right part of the character for 提 *ti* is the character 是 *shi*, made up of the modern version of the ancient pictograph for the sun, 日 *ri*, over 正 *zheng*, which means "correct," in the sense of "correct in the light of day." 是 is also the character for a variant of "to be," or "yes."

正 is also the generational name or middle name given to myself, my siblings, and indeed all first cousins of the same generation in the Mao family. A traditional, extended Chinese family could consist of three or four generations. To distinguish who is an uncle or who is a nephew, these generational middle names provide a guide to proper behavior.

Branding

Another aspect of promotion that successful innovators often leverage is branding. By that I mean that they develop and uphold a consistent theme and a respected performance standard. By communicating the common strategic intent behind different ideas, projects, and accomplishments, they differentiate their work, show how the individual pieces tie together, and more clearly communicate value. They inspire confidence. Clear branding is important when presenting to venture capitalists, executives, or the public. But it's important in a wider respect, too. Personal, project, and organizational brands are always connected. What we do in one sphere impacts others.

In the corporate world, I've met a number of very creative and productive people who were determined to bring about change and create value, yet were content to do so behind the scenes. They took great satisfaction in knowing that they made a difference, yet because they did not see themselves as future leaders or corporate executives, they never clarified the important role that they played. Many times, they even stepped back and let others reap the rewards of their hard work. I think the future needs leaders and executives with this creative, improvement-driven mind-set, so I always urge people not to shy away from clearly communicating the value of their personal brand

and the contributions they have made for their organization's success. That's not to say that someone should leverage the successful efforts of the team to promote themselves. I think it's critically important for long-term success to give credit where credit is due, a topic I will get back to later in the chapter.

The Importance of Establishing a Baseline for Innovation

I've found that many people don't take the time to understand, capture, and communicate the business impact of their work. Maybe they assume that important people already know their record and recognize their value. I don't think that's a fair assumption, though. I believe that we need to establish a "baseline" to promote the business value of what we are changing or improving with facts and data.

We never know when we'll encounter a good idea. And when we do, we usually attack it with a "laser focus." By the time we finish implementing, though, we've already changed our environment so much that we can't provide data on the situation before we went about improving it! It's like losing 50 pounds and not having a "before" picture! A big part of promotion is showing the "before" and the "after." Therefore, it's always smart to have a baseline measurement in place so when that good idea strikes, we can hit the ground running. The other benefit of a good baseline measurement is that it can actually generate good ideas. When people really see how long it takes to do something or how much it costs or the amount of rework involved, it generates the creative problem-solving mind-set that is behind so many innovations.

There are two kinds of metrics that we want to establish as our baselines. The first are our own operational management metrics— how many units of work we process, how long it takes, the number of errors encountered, productivity, cycle-time, and so on. The other type of metrics we need are business-focused. They demonstrate the impact of our work on revenue, expenses, customer satisfaction, unit costs for business transactions, or some other tangible, business-focused result.

Promoting Our Innovation Ideas

As I've said before, when it comes to communication and promotion, few corporate functions are more challenged than IT infrastructure. The eyes of business decision makers quickly glaze over when technical folks launch into the details and acronyms associated with their ideas. The spell is typically broken only when the word *dollars* is heard, and then suddenly executive attention is rapt. Many times, infrastructure folks—and others too—fill those precious few moments of attention with detail about what their idea will cost. Successful innovators communicate in terms of business value, what their ideas will gain, save, or achieve. This is true whether we're pitching ideas to corporate decision makers, venture capitalists, or potential customers.

I often meet with a variety of vendors to learn about their newest and planned products. Surprisingly often, I come across a vendor that has a fascinating and innovative offering, yet has difficulty articulating the value proposition of their offering in a business context. Sure, they talk about saving money or time or some other generic benefit. Yet their pitch is usually focused on the details of their product, not on the total costs and benefits to the business. For example, vendors will certainly provide information regarding licensing and other costs that they charge, but they sometimes seem oblivious about other transition-related costs that the business would obviously need to incur in order to leverage their product. Even the best pitch cannot account for everything, but a good one accounts for as much as possible. It speaks to business decision makers about their interests, in their language, crisply and clearly articulating why they should care. This doesn't require a fancy slide deck, as Dr. Eugene Chan, founder of the DNA Medicine Institute, will attest:

> I was filing my first patent for my first company, and my patent lawyer just happened to say, hey, I know this guy who invests in companies. So, I arranged to meet him and actually forgot my slides! I just drew out the idea on his yellow note pad, and right away he said, "Ok, I'll put in $300,000." I thought, Wow, okay, what should I do now?" It was fantastic! I guess there's always an element of luck.

I won't argue that luck may have helped Eugene get an audience with this investor, but I'm quite certain that it was Eugene's ability to clearly and convincingly convey the value proposition of his idea that earned him the investment.

As Jim Phalen, executive vice president of State Street, put it:

> Big companies are good at problem-solving. If there's an issue, you can probably galvanize an army to solve it. But new ideas often get lost or overwhelmed by the culture. Sometimes the management structure just kills it. Sometimes there's just not a good process for moving it forward. A lot of ideas get killed because of perception—hey, they didn't approve my product idea last year and I was only asking for $1 million. You're going to need $10 million? Forget it. But the $10 million idea may be better than the $1 million idea. Figure out what the issue was with the $1 million idea; why couldn't they make a case? If you believe strongly in your idea, take it forward.

The ideal, of course, is to not even need funding in the first place. We leverage our asset Life Cycle Management process—which is to always replace older technologies with the most current version of the technologies before the end of any asset's life cycle. This is a way of making a capital investment that typically reduces operating expense at the same time. It allows us to self-fund many projects. Before the useful life of our technology asset ends, we get ready with a replacement that is better, cheaper, and consistent with our technology blueprint. Most of the time, the new technology will not increase our operating expenses. In fact, expenses are usually reduced, because the more innovative solution is also more cost-effective. We get more for less. Sometimes, growth requirements consume the difference, although it's still transparent to the business. We're able to provide more capacity and improved performance at the same cost. Other times, we return a significant amount of our budget savings back to the organization, as demonstrating savings is key to effective promotion. And a third option is to reinvest the savings in another area where the payback period might take more than a single budget cycle. This technique of self-funding innovation through asset Life Cycle Management can just as easily be applied to areas other than infrastructure. It requires that innovators, or those leading them, have a good grasp of their financial baselines and the impact that their idea can have on their annual forecast.

Sometimes, self-funding just isn't possible. An understanding of the financial impact and a projected ROI (return on investment) or payback period will provide the firmest foundation for obtaining funding and staffing for innovative initiatives. Metrics that forecast the expected improvements will demonstrate a solid focus on results. Not all improvement ideas can be directly translated to increase revenue or reduce expenses, of course. And the more innovative the proposal, the less predictable the results. However, we try to get as close as we can to some measure of expected business value, whether it's in terms of cycle time, customer satisfaction, risk reduction, or some other important measure.

Even in organizations where special funding has been set aside for experimental projects, we're still potentially competing against other good ideas, so the more concrete we can be about our expected benefits, the better. This doesn't necessarily mean that only projects with short-term tangible benefits get funded. Companies are increasingly recognizing the value of innovation project portfolios that deliver over multiple time horizons. However, projects with short-term tangible benefits are far less likely to be rejected, especially if they also have even greater long-term potential. So successful innovators think in the long term, but do their best to deliver in the short term. Whenever possible, they structure their proposal in a way that demonstrates and delivers tangible benefits as early as possible. While some innovative ideas can be translated into short-term benefits and some cannot, virtually all will have a future potential that's either difficult or impossible to predict. That's the nature of innovation! So, innovators are always in a situation where they need to consider the best way to communicate that potential.

Dr. Eugene Chan, the medical innovator, has encountered the challenge many times in his own business and offers some great some advice through this story:

You really need to think about the right way to communicate about something that people haven't experienced yet. Everyone knows what it means to buy a diagnostic device because it measures the one thing they're interested in. But, if it actually measures ten things and gives them ten values, and also provides a diagnosis or predicts their physical state, that's very different. So, I have some business students working on a small project for me to figure out which of the two dozen or so tests is the best one for people to get started on. Maybe there's a disease people are managing and we can provide a really valuable test for them. That way we don't have to depend on a whole educational program that says, hey this is a completely brand new device and works differently in this way. I think once people start actually using this, they'll figure out the new features pretty soon afterward.

I think we'll also have help getting the message out because of the partners we're funded by. In 2015, our technology will be up on the NASA Space Station and in the National Institute of Health. They're backing our project and are incredibly supportive. If you watch Star Trek, you know about the Tricorder, so the folks at NASA were absolutely among the first to be on board with this.

There's no formula to use for promoting potential—it's a judgment call based on the specific decision makers, culture, appetite for risk, and many other factors. There's no need to minimize it, just a need to be thoughtful about what promises our proposal may imply. Now, I'm rarely, if ever, considered a conservative person. But this is one area where I'm often more realistic than others. I don't like to promise something that I may not be able to deliver. That's why I work very hard to take great ideas and find ways to get value from them early on, while building our way toward that greater, longer-term potential. When I don't know what I can reasonably deliver, my first proposal is a study or proof-of-concept or a pilot, which is a much smaller project. That gives the team the resources we need to do some research and experimentation in order to get to a closer estimate of what's possible and by when.

Some organizations formalize a similar process where funds are earmarked for limited initial funding to promising ideas. This allows the team to test their assumptions and more accurately assess potential through studies and experimentation. Ideas that are thus validated can then proceed through another funded stage as the real costs, benefits, and potential become increasingly clear.

Unfortunately, some organizations put their innovation projects through the same program management mill that traditional projects undergo. That can create issues since the usual role of program management is to measure progress to already-established expectations, not to reassess expectations after each stage.

It's clear that corporate innovators need to employ sound judgment to ensure that legacy processes—or inappropriate processes—don't slow or prevent progress. It's important that we have a good understanding of current processes and expectations (managing expectations is an essential aspect of effective promotion) and are able to anticipate what the potential issues and challenges might be. Then we can constructively address questions and potential concerns up front, rather than wind up in a defensive position later.

Creating a Promotion Plan

Once an idea becomes a project, a marketing and communications plan should be developed. A common plan format addresses these important choices:

- Audience: Who will we choose to communicate with?
- Timing: When will we choose to communicate?
- Content: What will we choose to communicate?
- Method: How will we choose to communicate?
- Approach: What attitude will we choose to communicate effectively?

It's important to consider the impact and role of trends such as mobile computing, analytics, and social media in each of the above. We can leverage advances in social media and related technologies to enhance awareness, interest, and engagement. In the past, promotion was largely a one-way broadcast. Information was "pushed out" using very traditional channels. Social media has significantly changed that by creating wide-open spaces for public conversations. Very direct message targeting is possible using advances such as analytics and location-awareness. This increases opportunities as well as the risks, especially in terms of brand promotion.

Chef Ming Tsai has an interesting take on the power of social media. He told me this story:

> I decided to open a new restaurant called Blue Dragon that we planned to open in February in Boston. This was a great move for me, for employees, and the company. But to be honest—I got too much press about the new restaurant too early. I didn't want to announce it until the end of December, but people saw me in the neighborhood and started speculating and found out that I had gotten a liquor license. People started writing and tweeting about it. We got a fantastic pre-opening, but we weren't going to open our doors for another two and a half months. I didn't think people were going to forget about us, but once the word is out there, you have to take advantage of it. We wanted to keep this story alive, so we turned to social media and kept the interest up. Funny, once people saw me talking about Blue Dragon, they said, "Yeah, we've got to get back to Blue Ginger!" You know, it all plays a part, which is a good thing.

As we develop our communications plan, we need to carefully consider the different audiences and stakeholders we will communicate with. Poor promotion can generate resistance or negative press and impact our ability to succeed. Are we telling others our plans? Or are we asking for input? How are questions and concerns communicated and addressed? How are different and perhaps even better ideas handled? The answers to these questions, and others like them, often mean the difference between generating enthusiasm and creating opposition. Since both of these can spread very quickly, the better we are at managing how we are perceived, the more success we will have. Communications that are open, inclusive, and responsive tend to dissolve resistance and invite support.

When John Swainson took over as CEO at CA Technologies (formerly Computer Associates), the company was in trouble. By the time John left CA, it had not only fully recovered but had regained its industry leadership. When I asked John how he managed to achieve this transformation, he was characteristically modest, yet identified the role of an effective communications plan:

> Cultures get destroyed quickly but take a long time to rebuild, particularly after they have been damaged. What we did (after I joined CA) was ultimately restore people's trust in the management team and the company's management processes. It was not any one big thing but rather a whole series of small things, delivering on what we said we were going to do and just sort of keeping at it and keeping at it and keeping at it—in my case for five years. We did a lot of communicating with people, we did a lot of town hall meetings, we did quarterly webcasts, we did blogs, e-mails, we did a lot of things. Mostly, we told people what we were trying to do. We gave them regular feedback on what was happening and gave them progress reports. And ultimately they saw that most of the time, what we said was going to happen was happening, and their confidence was restored.

As John indicates, communicating plans and results is a key element of success in any transformation or project. Even the most successful results can easily go unnoticed given the size and complexity of many organizations. As innovators, we can't assume that people see and understand them. We need to connect the dots. When we want someone else to see the value of our solution, we should make that as easy for them as we possibly can. We need to do that in a way that reflects the perspective of those to whom we're communicating, rather than our own perspective. This is much more difficult to do than most people realize. In fact, it's not a practice that I see demonstrated very often. Our target audience shouldn't have to understand how *we* see the world to recognize how our solution brings value to them. We need to understand how *they* see the world, and how our solution fits into it. The ability to listen well to and understand the people with whom we want to communicate *before* we begin communicating is an essential component of this.

Developing a clear, consistent message that reflects the interests of our different stakeholders requires planning, focus, and careful execution. John Thompson, CEO of Virtual Instruments and former CEO of Symantec, relays what he calls an "uncanny experience" during a trip to Japan when the news media there:

> . . . talked about how Symantec stock price was up 10 percent for the day based upon the strength of their announcement with AT&T, an announcement that I didn't know anything about. So I picked up the phone and I called the corporate PR leader to ask what we had announced that day with AT&T. And he said, well, gee, I don't know, we should find out about it. I said, If you are the corporate PR leader, how could you not know what happened? Well, the discovery was that we had communications spread across the company and if you were in Europe, you did it one way, if you were in the United States, you did it another way, if you were in a business unit, you did it one way, if you were in the field team, you did it in another way. So we hired a colleague of mine from IBM, who was a very, very good communications leader and consolidated all communications under him. Whether it was external or internal, whether it was a customer or press or investors, he had all the words that were to be spoken about the company. Internally or externally, it would all flow through him. And it was after he was put in place that we started to promote the idea that Symantec was in fact the world leader in security. And the rest is basically history.

The principles illustrated in John's story apply whether we are communicating internally to colleagues or superiors or externally to the wide world.

Developing and executing a well-thought-out communications plan speeds and simplifies progress for innovators. It anticipates and avoids misunderstandings, and it generates interest and enthusiasm. Yet it's important that we remember that even the best plan cannot take the place of the other essential element of an effective promotion strategy—the passionate and tightly crafted value statement.

Using Industry Awards and Recognition

Industry recognition enhances our brand and competitive position and also rewards and inspires our people. After our storage team at State Street implemented a new storage technology to consolidate and virtualize our massive library of e-mail files, we entered a storage industry award competition, and we received a notification that our company was among the few finalists. We sent the chief engineer and the manager of the storage group to the awards ceremony. The engineer took the stage with the other finalists and awaited the announcement of the winner—and it was us! This young man was thrilled to accept the award on behalf of our State Street team. On his way back, he sent me a note saying, "Madge, it was such a thrilling feeling when I was on stage—I am already working on our next storage award." At that moment, I realized that receiving outside recognition was not only great for our company, but also a huge motivator for my team. Team members are proud to say, "I was part of that." It inspires everyone and promotes the value of innovation.

I like to say that professional sales people are not the only people who need great sales and communication skills. Everyone involved in the process of innovation needs to seek out opportunities for promotion, continually attempting to gain support and spark interest. And once a new initiative has been successfully implemented, industry awards can serve as additional proof of the value it can deliver. They benchmark our progress against our peers and communicate and celebrate success internally and externally.

Several years ago, my team was chosen as one of the finalists for an award being given in the United Kingdom. It was a big deal and my European Regional Manager and I made plans to attend the formal awards dinner and ceremony. I also invited my former manager, Joe Antonellis, who was living in London. He had by then become vice chairman, head of all State Street business for Europe, Africa, and Asia-Pacific. At his suggestion, I extended invitations to all of the top business executives in our U.K. office to join us. The awards dinner was a great evening. It gave us a chance to get to know the business executives a lot better. Enjoying a celebratory evening with them and their spouses allowed us to bond and establish relationships. Throughout the dinner, they were interested in learning about our nominated project and they quickly recognized the value and advantage it would bring to State Street in Europe. We were one of the top three winners for that category, and State Street's name was on the board shining along with the other two winners. The evening gave us an unparalleled opportunity to establish our brand among all the attendees and beyond, and to communicate our value to State Street's top executives in the United Kingdom.

Promote—Don't Brag

As I hope I've made clear in the preceding pages, all aspiring innovators need to learn how to articulate and communicate their ideas in order to promote innovation. This is not to be confused with bragging—"blowing your own horn," as that former boss of mine put it. We must do it in a way that is acceptable to the norms of behavior of the corporate culture, does not offend our colleagues, and is provable. We should make both colleagues and superiors aware of the value innovation can bring to the company, in a businesslike manner. We have to learn how to package our accomplishments and include relevant metrics and proofs of strategic compatibility, and then to communicate them both internally and externally when the time is right.

Opportunities to Promote

As important as promotion is, endlessly communicating benefits can be counterproductive. We need to choose our timing carefully. Our goal is to ensure that people know about—and understand the value of—the benefits that matter to them. Communicating that value and establishing credibility is vitally important, but we also want to demonstrate that we understand their needs by not wasting their time, monopolizing their attention, or telling them what they already know.

Extremely effective promoters view every interaction with executives, staff, colleagues, and customers as an opportunity to promote. They keep it short and sweet, but they don't let a good opportunity pass them by. For example, at State Street, as a general courtesy, most executives would say, "Hi, Madge! How are you doing?" when they passed by me or we met in the elevator or parking garage. Instead of just replying "Very well, thank you," I would take that opportunity to tell them that we had just received an award from whatever industry or organization had most recently honored us. Most of the time, they would respond with great enthusiasm, asking about the award and what we did to earn it.

Executives have an essential role in promotion. Their public support makes a great deal of difference. It honors the work that has already been done, and inspires others to succeed as well. Listen to what Tom Mendoza, vice chairman of NetApp does every day:

> I wanted a very positive culture, so one of the things I started doing way back in 1994, right after I got to NetApp, was try to catch someone doing something *right*. I had been in many environments where people were always looking for what was wrong—but never in their group, by the way, always in someone else's group. Instead, I wanted a "thank-you culture." I don't think you can say "thank you" enough. I feel that if people know they are respected and appreciated, they will do almost anything for you, and that's part of creating the sort of safe culture leads to a lot of good new ideas.
>
> So, when I see someone doing something right, or if anyone at NetApp sees somebody do something extraordinary, whether it's helping a customer or helping a colleague, or just helping society, they send me an e-mail and I make a phone call. We log all those calls. I make about ten of them a day, and I make them seven days a week—wherever I am in the world I continue to make those calls. When I got to NetApp there were thirty-two of us; now we number more than 14,000,

but people still hear about it when someone in the company they know gets a call from me. They always ask: "Why did he call you?"

Success stories are always a great way to demonstrate value, and innovators should cultivate and communicate them. Tarkan Maner, previous CEO of Wyse Technology, serial entrepreneur, and investor, describes an experience he had several years ago when first venturing into one of his great passions—bringing Internet access to remote areas of the world:

We had written a case study about how we brought Internet access to villages in several emerging markets, and we showed pictures of children seeing and using the Internet for the first time. Our team was focused on providing success for customers, and we wanted to share the great results. It was a popular story and people in the media jumped on it, resulting in many unique stories in the press and various outlets. In just two months, we were on the cover of the *New York Times*, *Wall Street Journal*, and a few other leading publications. We couldn't believe it!

Tarkan was able to paint a very dramatic picture of his achievement. He communicated it effectively, and his story spread around the world. Even if all of our achievements are not quite as dramatic or world-changing—although I believe many of them can be—we need to become as effective as we can in the art of promotion. Here are three different levels with which we can estimate our own skills in this area.

Promote: Levels of Effectiveness

Level One: Creates Uncertainty

At Level One we have little or no focus on ensuring the value and brand are clearly communicated. Instead, we create uncertainty about it. We fail to gain necessary buy-in and support. Nor are we able to achieve appropriate recognition of potential and actual benefits.

Level Two: Creates Understanding

At Level Two we are able to clearly communicate the value proposition and secure funding and buy-in. We use regular and reliable channels to build awareness, knowledge, and interest. We are deliberate about measuring and communicating results.

Level Three: Creates Excitement

Level Three people are master promoters who create buzz and ensure endorsement by appealing to the interests of others. We never assume the message is already out there or understood. We leverage every opportunity to educate others, and we generate interest and enthusiasm (e.g., elevator pitches, awards). We benchmark against industry and differentiate brand and strategic value as well as results.

Promoting State Street's Environmental Sustainability and Green Programs

In 2001, State Street management prepared to build an enormous global enterprise data center. At the time, worldwide environmental sustainability initiatives were not yet a part of most corporate cultures. However, as a believer in preserving natural resources—and equally as important, preserving profit—I had long focused on reducing consumption of electricity and water.

This may have had something to do with my having grown up in China, where electricity was very expensive. As we grew up, we made a habit of conservation, because there wasn't much, and so we didn't want to waste such a precious resource. And in Hong Kong, when I was there, there was always a shortage of water. The city water was always shut off before lunch, and not turned on again until late afternoon before dinner. As a result, most households had a water tank to collect enough for urgent needs.

In America, many years later, my team of engineers and technologists designed the data center with the same sort of optimization and efficiency in mind. In fact, in creating our Technology Infrastructure Blueprint, we had already positioned ourselves for energy efficiency and conservation, with official standards in place for our technology environmental sustainability program, our efficiency program, and our design for the global data center infrastructure. State Street received twelve Green IT industry awards for its innovative efforts in sustainability and for its green initiatives. All the awards were for our innovative solutions backed by actual metrics to demonstrate our results. The awards stand as a great example of the positive impact that recognition within the industry can have. After all our hard work in this area, our team was gratified to be recognized for its efforts, State Street's employees were proud of the company as a whole, and the company's customers were pleased to know that State Street took sustainability seriously.

We started our formal efficiency and optimization program with the intention of lowering our operating expenses, lowering the unit cost of each technology infrastructure area, and reducing our consumption of resources. The program was so successful that State Street's business growth benefited for years to come.

The program focused on three major areas:

1. Culture and Communications
2. Method and Technology
3. Consumption Control

Culture and Communications

To begin, we established a structured management system capable of driving the program throughout the entire organization. With well-defined program goals, we formed an executive committee consisting of the senior leaders in Global Infrastructure Service. Then, we appointed a program lead and assembled work groups composed of chief engineers and engineers from each functional area. These engineers helped draw, define, and document our overall blueprint, and they laid out detailed project plans phase by phase. The team also defined the key metrics we wanted to measure and monitor and communicated them using an executive dashboard.

We also conducted regular town hall and functional area meetings to communicate the status and progress of the plan and the accomplishments of every employee. Further, we created a website with information about the program and news regarding our accomplishments.

Promoting this program through a clear and passionate message was one critical factor in its success. Inspiring everyone by benchmarking our achievements against our competitors was another. And we continued to compete for awards and recognition around the world. Altogether we created a culture of urgency and focus on change that reverberated throughout the entire organization.

Method and Technology

Our promotional plan also sought to leverage all available technologies and processes to accelerate our green program. Our Zero Footprint, Maximum Impact™ solution reduced the number of new datacenters we would have to construct and maintain. And we utilized virtualization for every key infrastructure component to reduce the amount of physical hardware and data center space. By this I mean we managed a group of technology infrastructure components, like servers, storage, and middleware, into one environment. This in turn increased asset utilization, which together reduced the data center space, utility costs such as electricity and water, and cost of support staff. Virtualization, in fact, was a major factor in our successful Green program.

We even pulled in cold air during the winter to help cool down the data centers, instead of only using air conditioning. And we pulled hot air out of the data centers to lower their temperature, significantly reducing their consumption of electricity.

Consumption Control

Most aspects of consumption control can be inexpensive and easy to accomplish—when the proper culture and attitude exist. (Some aspects, such as storage consumption, are not so easy to control.) To begin, we focused on power management, ensuring that all rooms had automatic lights. Then we implemented a new technology that allowed us to start or shut down the desktop computers when the system needed to update, or for security reasons, or when the computer were not in use. In this way, we could save electricity. We also purchased hardware with lower voltage requirements, supported a work from home program, championed hybrid cars, replaced all old monitors with flat screens, and recycled obsolete technology equipment and media. We instituted video-conferencing, too, reducing the travel costs associated with face-to-face meetings and lowering the company's carbon footprint. We also implemented usage-based chargeback, providing business areas with useful and detailed information about the IT infrastructure resources that they used each month. This gave business managers insight into what was driving their IT infrastructure costs. Once they understood that, they could put controls into place to minimize unnecessary usage.

Most of our environmental sustainability initiatives were completed before the major focus on "green" that we see all around us today. We were early innovators in these efforts, and one side benefit I should mention was that our achievements in this area made State Street even more visible and popular. Many of our new hires were excited to be working for a company that took such a serious interest in sustainability and had already accomplished so much. All of us were gratified by the way we had promoted steps that every individual could take to help reduce our company's overall impact on the environment!

Promote—Concrete Steps for Putting This Discipline into Action

Individual

To promote ourselves and our work, we should learn to "blow our own horn," but in a way that cannot be mistaken as bragging. The most effective method is through metrics. As a matter of course, when we innovate, we should establish a baseline to which we reference and compare our new and improved results. In effect, we provide before and after pictures as a way of showing how our innovation is improving things.

We should always communicate our ideas—and our accomplishments—in terms of business value. What will our ideas gain, save, or achieve? When we answer these questions in our presentations, we earn the attention our audience, whether it be our company's decision makers, venture capitalists, or potential customers. Once an idea does become a project, we should develop a marketing and communications plan to support it.

Team and Organization

Teams and organizations, like individuals, should also be referencing metrics and business value in promoting their work. Teams can make a policy of promoting ideas and solutions through the lifecycle of their projects. First, we promote in an effort to get funding and staff, then to garner support and buy-in, then to encourage awareness and interest. Finally, when our vision becomes a reality, we promote to demonstrate the value and benefits of our work. Throughout, we should be thinking long term, but striving to deliver short-term benefits as early as possible—and promoting that fact.

Organizations can formalize a process where money is earmarked for limited initial funding of promising ideas, allowing teams to test assumptions and potential through smaller studies and experimentation. Ideas that prove promising can then move to another funded stage as the real costs and potential benefits become clear.

Organizations should encourage teams to benchmark and apply for industry awards and recognition. Both provide a great way to promote a company's innovation accomplishments and to motivate teams and individuals to even greater achievements.

How to Promote

✓ Promote with passion and energy. Passion is contagious

✓ Constantly assess each moment as an opportunity to promote

✓ Focus on promotional details—why, how, whom, when, where, and what to promote

✓ Create fact-based promotion. Benchmark against industry for recognition and awards

✓ Always have a three-minute elevator speech ready—simple and clear

✓ Promote widely. Never assume that people have already heard the message

✓ Promote your brand clearly based on delivering customer value and benefits, and make sure people understand its prospective value

✓ Focus on the value to your customers' and users' business interests—not just your product's functions/features

✓ Everyone should acquire the skills for promotion

連

Chapter 5

Connect

The discipline of *Connect* has two dimensions: one is about relationships and the human connections we make with the people we work with and live with. The other relates to connecting to the larger realities of our businesses: vision, strategy, processes, market trends, and more—and also connecting across industries and across disciplines—as we move down our innovator's path.

Connection in the interpersonal sense is one of the first things we experience as soon as we are born as our parents reach out to us and hold us in their arms. In those earliest moments of infant life, we form a connection to our parents. This connection and the nurturing that goes along with it is the major source of our mental and physical growth. As we begin to grow up, our connections broaden to include other children, friends, relatives, and other people around us. There is little doubt that, from the beginning, we all have basic instincts and skills needed for connecting with others. At the same time, and to varying degrees, as we learn how to connect, we also learn how to treat people the way we would like to be treated.

In our businesses, as in our personal lives, connections and relationships are vitally important. Connections we make internally as well as externally are critical to our success as individuals as well as the success of teams, and of organizations as a whole.

John Swainson, the president of Dell Software, concurs:

> Most innovations are not the creations of one person. There are some exceptions obviously, but most innovations are collective accomplishments, where a lot of people put a lot of things together. Yes, certainly, a design genius like Steve Jobs brought insight into how Apple products ought to be positioned and packaged, but it took many, many, many people to get those products to the point where Steve's insight could be translated into reality.

It's easy to see why connections are important. People do business with those they know and trust. With modern globalization, the benefits from collaboration are greater today than ever before, making our connections even more important. Using them, we can leverage everyone else's good ideas and experiences to make our ideas even better. And others can do the same, leveraging ours.

We all gain greater momentum in innovation by leveraging relationships and connections with customers, partners, vendors, professional colleagues and friends, acquaintances, internal teams, and individuals. Now, we can challenge each other and learn from each other—and the result from collaboration in most cases will be a win-win-win solution to any problem we encounter. Each party wins, and together, we all win.

Connect 連 *Lian*
The character for *lian* is composed of two elements that represent forms of transportation—車 *che*, meaning "a cart," or "car," on the right, and "a boat" underneath and to the left. Thus, in traditional Chinese, the term connotes speed, by all

means possible, for connecting with people, communicating outward, making connections, and putting two and two together quickly.

The character can also imply "catch," or "fit," and also conveys 同心同意 *tongxin tongyi*, a modern Chinese term, literally meaning "same mind, same intention." People connect first, and then they may begin to see things the same way, or develop the same intentions. It does not always happen right away, and that's where leadership comes in. Effective leadership makes it possible for people to connect (on a high level), but also to connect with many persons (across a broad plain), which also expands one's personal horizon.

連結 *lianjie*, 連接 *lianjie* are both extensions of the idea of connecting. Finally, using the characters 感同身受, or said to have a common bond, in the sense of two persons feeling the same resonance. In the corporate world, this sense of two or more persons "in tune" with the same vibrations can be extrapolated to include other sensitivities—such as becoming one with corporate strategy, your customers' needs, and the industry as a whole.

Dr. Tenley Albright, director of MIT Collaborative Initiatives, is an iconic innovation leader who has mastered the art of connecting people from many different industries, institutions, organizations, professions, generations, countries, and so on to solve common issues. When she first started her MIT Collaborative Initiative—Module 5—she invited seventy people to convene for a brainstorming session. These people were from our military services (Army, Navy, Air Force, Marines), financial services, technology companies, consumer goods, manufacturing, health care, universities, entrepreneurs, publishing, and more. Her experience told her that people from different backgrounds would take a fresh look at problems and would be able to provide many more new and innovative ways of resolving them. Tenley recognized this need early on, while still a student:

I was always concerned at Harvard Medical School about how hard it was to know all the things that were going on. There was so much wonderful work going on, but I found that the people in labs next to each other, or in buildings next to each other, didn't know what their colleagues were doing. And that made me feel that we had to do something about connecting. There was so much good, individual research being done, but it was not being brought together. I thought all work would benefit if we could bring people together. I knew all their efforts could become quite a bit stronger if they join hands or arms or minds. And based on my feelings about that and my feelings that if you get people together from very different perspectives—people who wouldn't ordinarily meet each other—but are at the very top of their own field, then you might be able to improve something or break a logjam. Although we need experts in every field, very often they reach a plateau of sorts and stop moving upwards. Maybe they can't move ahead on their own anymore and need an infusion of new ideas from a different field? To me it's a little bit like a plant. You can give it water, and it will only grow so much. But if you give it other nutrients, like ideas from different sources, it will grow in ways no one could have imagined.

As Tenley knew, the list of people, organizations, and entities with whom we need to connect is a full one. We have to stay connected to people with whom we work: our team members, our colleagues, our bosses. We need to connect with other teams in the company so we'll know about any initiatives they might have underway. We need to stay closely connected to our business partners and our vendors so that we'll be the first to hear about their new offerings, and they'll be the first to hear about our coming needs. We have to stay connected to our competitors, so we know how to position ourselves competitively. In addition, we need to connect globally with other industries and sectors to leverage other ideas and expertise. The list of connections goes on and on.

As I said earlier, people prefer to do business with people they know and trust. We all are more likely to go the extra mile for people with whom we have positive relationships and mutual respect. In Chapter 1, *Listen*, I mentioned that I had worked with the CEO of one of State Street's largest vendors to dramatically improve the terms of a very problematic contract. There are many stories like that about vendors coming through when the chips were down! When we treat vendors fairly and honorably, they can truly become our strategic partners. And under the right circumstance, such as the one Tarkan Maner, previous CEO of Wyse Technology, serial entrepreneur, and investor, describes, they can even be our "Santa Claus":

My mother always told me, "Love life and love people." My sister and I grew up believing that. I like to give everybody a chance with trust. Sometimes you might get hurt, but what is the point of living otherwise? I've learned that you have to be prudent in relationships, but you should still give everyone a chance. Do we get betrayed, and do we sometimes get let down? Yes, of course. But for every person who let me down, I have many, many more amazing relationships to show for my taking a chance.

How does this work in business? I'll tell you. I went to a meeting with a customer today—a really great, really charming person. But his company is having a lot of problems, many problems. Their revenue is way down and they just let go of 11,000 people. I know they have no money. But at the same time, I know they need to change their technology if they are going to survive. So I said to this customer, "I will give you the products you need for free. Keep using them, upgrade them, and when you have money, and the budget is back in shape, then you'll pay me. I'll be here—I am not going away. You are not going away."

We are doing great—we're very profitable. So I said, "I'll share this success with you." My customer said, "I'm so touched that you're doing this. You're like Santa Claus! You are never

going to go away, and we will be here with you." This is how
a relationship of trust works.

Not many of us are so fortunate to have Santa Claus as a vendor.
But all of us can develop mutually supportive relationships. The best
of these, naturally, take time, as both parties establish positive track
records, a body of common experience, and trust.

These are the kinds of connections we should value greatly, especially as they grow from beginnings as ordinary business relationships
into lasting connections, and as trust grows stronger with every interaction. It is often said that we live in a far more connected world than
ever before, but having 500+ friends on Facebook is not the same as
knowing we can count on someone with whom we've had positive
work experiences in the past. It's especially gratifying when such connections continue to grow stronger over time and in spite of geography.
As we all know, our business partners now can be sitting on the other
side of the world. Our customers may be in towns or cities we never
heard of before and need help learning to pronounce correctly!

Tom Mendoza of NetApp gives a great example of the benefit of
connection when it comes to customers—how a strong, trusting connection, in this case based on service, can keep the business relationship
strong and help it endure.

> You can never lead in every area of a product. But if your
> customers believe in you as a company, if they trust you
> because you were there when they had a problem and
> you made that problem go away, and they know that you'll
> work with them, well . . . the next person to come up with
> a better product feature, say, doesn't always get the next deal
> because your customer is thinking, "Yeah, I hear you, but I
> don't know you. I'm not sure how you are going to react
> when I have a problem. But I know how *they* react." So, it is
> so important to gain, keep, and not lose the trust of the cus-
> tomer, and it's something that requires a total company focus.

It's probably obvious by now that the discipline of *Promote*, which
I discussed in Chapter 4, can be put into practice and even made more

effective through the discipline of *Connect*. For innovators, the success of any major initiative will depend on our ability to connect with stakeholders and internal teams within the organization, and customers, vendors, and business partners outside. Those connections will inspire individuals and groups to buy in, and encourage them to challenge each other to do even better at their next opportunity. We also need to connect with each other's experience, keeping our eyes and our minds open to what we have learned and how each experience might relate to another. In a fascinating interview with *Wired* in 1996, Steve Jobs said,

> Creativity is just connecting things. When you ask creative people how they did something, they feel a little guilty because they didn't really do it, they just saw something. It seemed obvious to them after a while. That's because they were able to connect experiences they've had and synthesize new things. Unfortunately, that's too rare a commodity. A lot of people in our industry haven't had very diverse experiences. So they don't have enough dots to connect, and they end up with very linear solutions without a broad perspective on the problem. The broader one's understanding of the human experience, the better design we will have.[1]

This observation applies to innovative teams and organizations as well as to creative individuals. Focusing only on what is happening within our own walls is a mistake on many levels, and certainly not conducive to innovation. The more we connect—and the more broadly we connect—the more perspective we bring to our thinking and solutions.

Deborah Ancona, professor of management and director of the MIT Leadership Center, describes the concept of *X-Teams*, where the X stands for external:

[1] Gary Wolf, "Steve Jobs: The Next Insanely Great Thing," *Wired* 04.02, 1996, www.wired.com/wired/archive/4.02/jobs_pr.html.

If you look at most of the books on what makes for high-performing teams, the typical answer includes things like clear goals, clear roles, commitment, trust among members, good communication, and effective group processes. All of that is absolutely important. But it can also build impermeable boundaries and a kind of hubris.

You can't just connect inside the team, you really have to create large networks outside the team, across teams, within the organization, up the organization, and outside the organization with partners, with stakeholders, with people along the supply chain. You need people with connectivity—or an ability to just go out and talk to others in your core customer group, in the marketplace, in organizations that are doing things better than you are.

That ability to go outside, to go across the boundaries, to engage in external sense-making and ambassadorship—that's critical. All of that requires a very open system, a very externally oriented kind of team.

Our global teams and strategic partners can offer significant assistance and insight as we're planning for a change or innovation—or should be planning and just don't realize it yet. They can provide us with a more complete perspective and share lessons learned from similar experiences. I always connected widely with others in my work at State Street, and it helped us resolve our issues, improve the quality of our services, and reduce costs. This approach also established a higher level of trust between different companies, which led to better partnerships. Also, by treating strategic partners as members of our extended staff, we fostered teamwork and collaboration among all team members, leading to renewed effort on the part of everyone, since we were now striving for a common goal.

Deborah continues:

There's a lot of potential for competitive advantage in managing the supply chain. And you can't manage it if you don't really understand it or know who is doing what and the value each piece provides. So, this notion of going outside, connecting outside, is resulting in executives taking themselves out of their comfort zone. For instance, there are top executives at Costco going into the villages in Central America. Why? Because they now have an interest in farming sustainability, because they are interested in safety of supply. If all of those farms go out of business, their supply of fruits and vegetables could disappear. Similarly, Coke is partnering with the World Wildlife Foundation, to deal with water. Companies are forging very different kinds of partnerships, thinking in an expanded view about different stakeholders along the supply chain, and networking with others who often see the world very differently.

Another interesting approach is Dean Kamen's notion of *coopertition*, a term coined to represent the ideals of cooperation and competition. Interacting positively when interests mesh, teams help each other, pool knowledge, and work together to some degree, even though they are at the same time in competition. In one famous example, a robotics competition sponsored by Dean required teams to help one another rebuild robots damaged in the event in order to get them ready for the next round of competition.

Although he doesn't use the word *coopertition*, Sam Palmisano takes the concept even further, seeing a future in which major organizations, in order to be successful, will cooperate with each other as much as they compete. Old boundaries that have existed between organizations, disciplines, governments, and even between leaders are already falling, and new and productive connections are being established everywhere.

Successful global leaders are taking advantage of the powerful new capabilities we have available. Seizing upon an instrumented, interconnected, and intelligent world enables any organization to take waste out, to give customers and communities what they want, to organize work differently. These leaders see themselves as collaborators. Competition is essential as a spur to innovation. But in a world of interdependent systems, competition needs to be complemented and tempered by collaboration across old boundaries: across academic disciplines, industries, and nations—and even among competitors. This applies to individual leadership styles, too. The most active and successful leaders today see themselves as part of global communities and peer groups. They listen as much as they speak. They are hungry to learn from other people, from colleagues and communities, even people they will never meet in person.

The ability to connect with others is one of the most essential "soft skills" a person can have. As I mentioned earlier, we all have that ability when we are infants and very young children. But often it doesn't last; many of us lose the skill as we grow older, especially as we enter the competitive world of business. Many of us also lose our appreciation of the impact connections can have on our lives, careers, and the ability to achieve our ultimate goals. We can be very task-focused in our jobs and miss important opportunities to reach out to others. Worse, in the course of our work, the intensity it often requires, and the pressure of deadlines, we may even unintentionally alienate the very people on whom we will someday need to rely. No matter how skilled and dedicated we are at our jobs, a great deal of our success is determined by the quality of our relationships with others. This, in turn, is a matter of the respect we show others, and the extent to which we practice emotional intelligence. As we discussed in Chapter 2, *Lead*, emotional intelligence allows us to empathize with others, to understand their needs, objectives, and concerns. Admiral Mullen provides a great example of the role that emotional intelligence and connection plays in our personal and professional success:

> As Congress is often pointing out, they really are the ones that decide where the money goes. We in the military are just giving them ideas about resourcing certain technologies or approaches. In my own . . . almost 20 years of experience with Congress, I have found—despite what might be portrayed in the press—that the vast majority of Congressmen and -women are very open to new ideas.

I've found that it's important to stay engaged with the Congressmen and -women and work with them. When we do that, they usually are very supportive. You have to stay connected on a frequent basis with both Members as well as their staffers. When I was a more junior admiral, I would deal more with the staffers than I did the principals, but as I became more senior, it was the opposite. One of the things I really tried to make sure I never did was forget the principals' staff. Like all of us, Congressmen and -women have an awful lot on their plate. I always stay in touch with the staffers because they are the ones that study the issue in detail and they are the ones that set the tables for their bosses.

Connect: Levels of Effectiveness

As I've done with the other disciplines, I'd like to share my observations on the different levels of Connect I have experienced and observed in my years in business. We connect with those around us at one of three basic levels. As in other chapters, we should make a go of determining what level we are operating at and what we need to do to get to the next one.

Level One: Stand-Alone

At Level One we exhibit a silo-type mentality. We remain isolated in our thinking, approach, and solutions. We may go through the motions of collaboration, but often with the intent of just getting it over with. (We call that *clobberation*; more about this phenomenon later.) This leader is purely transaction-focused and has not understood the importance of relationship building.

Level Two: Integrated

At Level Two we are well connected, and before making decisions, we weigh a wide range of input from a diverse group of stakeholders. We align ourselves and our initiatives with corporate strategy, or with existing or planned solutions. We seek and unify stakeholder perspectives to ensure alliances and create effective solutions. This leader makes sure to invest in long-term relationships.

Level Three: Intersected

At Level Three we consistently reach outside of our usual "circle of connectivity" to find and leverage innovative ideas and new ways of creating business value. We actively seek out diverse and seemingly unconnected industries, age groups, technologies, and more. We enjoy helping others to succeed. This leader establishes enduring partnerships through integrity, trust, and generosity.

The Connect Culture

In Asian culture, connections can be the most critical factor in a business's success. In China, where I grew up, a connection is more than a simple, transactional relationship. Connections can take years to cultivate and establish, and individuals and businesses need them to succeed. This manner of doing business has played a vital role in Asian commerce for thousands of years, overshadowing the practices of the modern business world, which is a relatively recent phenomenon. The culture still exists today, just as in centuries past, and merchants acquire new business by being properly connected and recommended by friends or relatives.

My brother and sisters and I observed the value of connections from the time we were very young. My parents always had many friends and relatives stopping by to visit us—almost every day. I don't remember very many times when we had dinner just by ourselves. The good thing was that we got to know many other people really well and enjoyed their company. Then, these people would bring their own friends, and also invite us to their homes. Connections were always being made. If we ate alone, my father would ask me and my siblings to tell him what happened to us during that day. We each tried to construct an interesting story about our friends and their parents and our activities for that day. It was his way of being connected with us and learning about the connections we were making ourselves.

By this time, my father had become the master of all captains and crews for a shipping company, and also for Shanghai harbor. Through his work, my parents got to know many people. In those years, workers in China didn't have vacation days. If they wanted to take time off, they had to resign from their company, and then find another job after their vacation!

My mother had a golden heart and was very generous and passionate about helping people in need. Even though she was a housewife, she became the equivalent of a "placement officer" for her vast number of acquaintances. When someone came to her for help, I often heard her say, "I know Mr. So and So, and Mr. So and So knows Mrs. Such and Such, and she needs a worker. . . ." In this way, she was usually able to find people jobs.

Sometimes, we children also got involved. I remember a friend of my parents once sought my mother's help for a business transaction with a company she had never dealt with before. We discovered that the father of one of my classmates was the head of the business that they wanted to connect with. So my classmate was able to introduce my parents to her parents, who in turn introduced them to the family seeking to do business. The outcome of all this connectedness was a successful business transaction that made everyone happy.

So we grew up understanding the critical nature of connections in our lives and our work. It comes naturally to me to treat customers as "honored guests" and vendors and suppliers as "strategic partners."

My parents always said that we must treat people as they personally liked to be treated. They also told us that we should not connect with people when we needed a favor for ourselves—that would be using people inappropriately. We should always make connections with the people we meet when we don't need anything from them, and we should always help them whenever we can. Then, when we need help, grateful people would reciprocate the favors.

With the culture and training I experienced while growing up, it became very natural for me to connect with the people I meet and always seek out the positive side of relationships, even if some of the people I am dealing with are not so nice or sincere.

Connect and Cooperate

As Dr. Tenley Albright and her work have shown us, connections have the effect of bringing us into a larger community where we are exposed to ideas and points of view that will probably be different from ours and new sources of information, all of which will help us find better ways of identifying solutions.

Remember that old story about the blind men and the elephant? Trying to identify the thing in front of them, each man touched a different part of the animal and so believed it to be something different: the man touching the trunk thought it was a snake; the leg became a pillar; the tail a rope, and so on. Imagine how quickly they could have figured it out if they had connected before trying to answer the question!

Related to the story about those poor men trying so ineffectively to solve the elephant problem is the unfortunate tendency for some of us to stay disconnected from those around us to the point of isolation. This can be seen in the case of individuals, teams, and business divisions and can give rise to "silo solutions." Many people become overwhelmed by the pressure of addressing multiple and often conflicting opinions. Rather than deal with the challenge, trying to avoid difficult interactions with others, they isolate themselves and their teams from others. This tendency usually ends up greatly oversimplifying the problem or the opportunity they are facing. And while this approach simplifies decision-making and action-taking, it eliminates all the advantages of collaboration. The result is that their solution becomes a "point solution" that perhaps deals with the immediate problem inside the silo, but doesn't help the organization as a whole and ends up adding complexity and cost. Connections, of course, mitigate the tendency toward silo solutions.

There is another form of unconnectedness that I need to talk about. I mentioned it earlier and it's called *clobberation*—a term coined by my chief of staff, Marcy Wintrub, that combines the words "clobber" and "collaboration." Clobberation occurs when a team leader goes through all the motions of collaboration—inviting us to all the right meetings, copying us on all the memos, adding our names to every document. But, in truth, they are not listening to our input—they really don't care about our ideas or concerns or proposed solutions. We leave their meetings feeling *clobbered* by their predefined and aggressively defended solution, not collaborated with to develop something we can all believe in. What makes this behavior even worse is that our names have been added to their documentation, making it appear that we have bought in to their silo solution.

Another common mistake is going to the opposite extreme—trying to address the needs and concerns of all stakeholders right away. That doesn't work either. Many people think that collaboration requires consensus. I don't believe that. I think successful collaboration requires leadership. A good leader listens to the requirements, suggestions, and concerns of team members and then synthesizes that input into the best possible solution, given the circumstances. Any open issues are recognized and a plan is put into place for addressing them going forward. Rather than working toward complete consensus, the leader finds a path forward that everyone can support.

Yes, connecting is about preserving relationships, increasing buy-in, and generating enthusiasm—and still being able to get a good solution out the door, on time and on budget.

Inventor and former Microsoft Chief Technology Officer, Nathan Myhrvold, addresses these issues directly—how the lack of connection can hamper innovation:

> Probably more start-ups and projects fail because of human issues than technology issues. People disagree. They can't communicate. They can't manage. So you have to understand the human side as well as the technological side. The ideal team is something that combines both. It's got some great ideas and great idea makers—brilliant people who can come up with ideas. And they have the right structure and management and the right human qualities so they're able to communicate with each other, manage the thing, and communicate with others as well. All those qualities are what really make us successful.

Connecting Strategy, Processes, and Systems

There are other layers of meaning in *Connect* we need to be aware of as we work, plan, and innovate: We need to make sure we are connected to larger realities, like the company's vision, or its mission, or its goals and long-term strategies. And while maintaining those connections, we have to stay connected to the requirements of day-to-day production as well. We also have to connect to the marketplace as a whole, so we can keep up with advances and trends in our industry.

When he was CEO of Symantec, John Thompson was very open to new ideas, as long as they were closely connected to the business's strategy:

> I think it's important in any organization, particularly in a tech organization, that innovation be allowed to bubble up from the bottom. And so the mantra at Symantec was that innovation would be driven from the smart people across the company. Whatever job you had, if you had a great idea, I would be open to listening to that great idea. And people knew that, so they were not bashful about sharing their point of view, and I was also equally unabashed with them if I had to say, "That one doesn't quite strike the hot button for us." Eventually they caught the drift that I was very much focused on being the leader in security, and therefore if they didn't have ideas around that, they might as well stay out of my office.

It's significant that John mentions innovation bubbling up from the bottom. There is an emerging trend in the use of processes and tools that solicit and welcome new ideas from all kinds of sources. Companies are increasingly inviting innovation ideas from employees at all levels, customers, and vendors, and not limiting themselves to what their "idea people" have to say.

Connecting with strategy applies to internal process and systems innovation as much as it does to product innovation. Most of us are very familiar with the ways in which silo-thinking can create inefficient and ineffective solutions. As customers, we have experienced being transferred from department to department with little continuity or progress on our problem or request. Sometimes the several customer reps we speak with on a single call almost seem to be working for different companies. Within an organization, we often see how point solutions can create problems for other functions, or at best do not help solve problems systemwide. For example, we've probably all seen situations where multiple solutions require similar data, yet each group organizes and formats their data in such starkly different ways that any connection is lost. The role of translating and synchronizing data across systems often falls to the unfortunate end-user that these systems have in common, subverting the whole intent of automation!

In addition to being inefficient, these practices can lead to unreliable data and certainly prevent real-time insight or consolidated reporting. Although they may appear to solve departmental problems in the very short term, they're often just shifting problems to other parts of the organization, and even compounding them. Solutions like these are much more likely to create complexity and cost than business value and competitive advantage. Innovators can solve immediate problems too, yet at their best they do so in a way that integrates rather than isolates solutions.

Dell Software's President John Swainson's remark earlier in the book remains relevant here. He said that the future of innovation will be about ways in which technologies get integrated together. "A lot of innovation happens because of the ability to connect different technologies together and the new capabilities that they enable."

Here's another example of skillful connection in innovation when discoveries and processes in one industry are applied to another. Who would have imagined that automobile manufacturing had relevance to surgical procedures? As Nathan Myhrvold points out:

> Car companies build cars with robots. Welding robots, in particular, weld the various pieces of steel together. That's pretty routine. Surgeons, on the other hand, haven't used robots until very recently. But there is an increasing use of specialized robots to do certain kinds of surgeries, particularly laparoscopic surgeries where you can use these little robot arms to fit inside a patient, making a smaller hole. So, you are applying an idea that was used in car factories, used for lots of other things,

and all of a sudden you are applying that in a brand-new area—surgery.

Ways to Connect

One of the most effective ways to begin making connections is to reach out to people in a way that makes them feel comfortable. Even creating a comfortable environment helps. If we can make people feel at home (relatively speaking of course) in the office, we are moving in the right direction.

Let's take a tip from Chef Ming Tsai and his restaurant business, where nurturing connections with both customers and employees is a critical part of success.

> Customers look at price, and they'll only come back if they think they are getting good value. Otherwise you'll just see them once a year for a birthday, and you can't survive on birthday and anniversary celebrations. You have to make sure that when they leave they're happy, and they're full, and they're feeling that they also received great *value*. That's when they come back. When they do, and you see them, and you welcome them, you feel like they're family and *they* feel like they're home. And this is true for your employees too. Feeling like a part of the family is a lot better than feeling like a worker. Here at Blue Ginger, we've produced nine marriages and ten kids. That's serious family!

Our offices are not like our homes, but what can we personally do in the workplace that creates a comfortable atmosphere where good business relationships and connections can be nurtured? Leaders have to like people, show that they care about them, and operate an open, friendly, and inspirational environment. People are most productive and creative when they are in an environment where there is no fear but instead inspiration and trust. The team would be most productive when they can share their ideas and collaborate with each other. Connections between team members can occur somewhat naturally, especially if the right people are recruited and the right kind of chemistry exists.

A diverse team can deliver a more comprehensive solution. Young people, not weighed down or prejudiced by experience, can offer fresh and interesting perspectives. They tend to see all the possibilities and opportunities instead of obstacles. They can be powerful drivers of innovation, as Admiral Mullen expresses it—

> I think the young in particular are almost naturally more innovative. They are not inhibited or restrained by life experiences, which with rare exception adults almost always are and more experienced people almost always are. (Of course, there are exceptions.) So if youth is just so much more unconstrained, how do we cultivate their spirit and their ideas and make them work with experience? A good leader is there for both the youthful and older team members to connect to. If the connection is not made, the young are going to go somewhere else to innovate, someplace where they are welcomed and their ideas and opinions sought.

Connecting with My Team

Although I was hired to oversee State Street's corporate technology infrastructure, it was several years before infrastructure functions in the company's global sites began reporting in to me. That was a very dramatic change for the organization, which was highly decentralized at the time. People who worked at site locations did not always view corporate functions with high regard. Besides being thought of as very United States–centric, corporate functions were sometimes considered slower, behind the times, and not as in touch with customer needs. With those kinds of prevailing attitudes, no sense of camaraderie could develop across geographical locations. When interactions did occur, especially between corporate and personnel at the site locations, it was usually because an issue of some sort had arisen and needed to be dealt with. As a result, relations were tense and people were wary about the new global model.

As soon as I could, I arranged a large-scale team meeting to bring together two layers of infrastructure managers reporting to me. I also invited several key partners from related functions, such as finance and procurement. All in all, we had about sixty people come together for two days. We knew this was our chance to change how people thought and felt about each other, so my support team spent hours just planning the table seating, as if this event were a wedding! We strategically mixed and matched, populating each table with people from very different functions and locations.

We put together our agenda with a light touch. Day ONE was about Ownership, Navigation, Escalation, the essential practices allowing individuals to deliver customer-focused service in a global organization. Day TWO was about Teamwork, World-Class Quality, and One Global Process, the commitments that bind people and teams together. We took great care to avoid making the event a corporate orientation session that told our global partners "this is how we do things here." In fact, we wanted the session to provide a unified global perspective, a first for all attendees. We filled each day with speakers, exercises, and plenty of time for people to get to know each other. They did. Preconceived assumptions and long-held resentments began melting away as people got to see that their counterparts were not so very different from them after all. It was a great, productive session that set the stage for a truly global organization.

At three in the afternoon on the final day, our CIO, Joe Antonellis, was scheduled to stop by. We decided to line up for a photograph so that he could join us when he arrived. One of the building staff offered to take the picture, and I busied myself organizing this large group into four neat rows. I had just finished when Joe walked in. "Come on over, Joe!" I called, motioning him to join us. As we stood by the group, I realized I had organized the rows so well that it was not at all clear where Joe and I would fit. He's as tall as I am small, so we stood there for a moment. Suddenly, Masood, our command center's shift manager, shouted out a suggestion, "Madge, why don't you and Joe get down on the floor?" There was a very uncomfortable silence for a moment as people thought about what he had just said. Without missing a beat, Steve, our availability management lead, called out with faux pity, "Well, it was nice working with you, Masood!" The room erupted in laughter just as Joe and I stepped into place and the camera clicked. Every person's face in the picture is filled with joy and laughter, none more so than Masood and Joe. It's the best picture ever and a powerful representation of connection. The team got hold of the digital file and made me a framed poster-sized copy that has hung on my wall ever since.

MIT Collaborative Initiatives and the Albright Challenge

I'd like to end the chapter with an examination of the MIT Collaborative Initiatives, an initiative cofounded by Dr. Tenley Albright, whom we met earlier in the chapter. She is, in my opinion, the master of getting together people from different industries, different backgrounds, and different age groups to find innovative ways to solve the world's most pressing problems.

> We need to change the way things are done—this statement is resonating around the globe. Our problems are more complex; our resources are fewer. Since its inception, MIT Collaborative Initiatives has been working quietly to support a change in the way we approach problems and manage complex, multidisciplinary, large-scale challenges.
>
> No longer can we be content keeping pockets of deep knowledge isolated from each other. We must reach across, connect, and create a larger body of shared experience to draw on. This type of collaboration, coupled with a systems-based approach and tools designed specifically to manage complex conceptual problems, can lead us to innovation.
>
> Based on this belief and a conviction that progress can move much faster if experts and organizations both within and outside of a given problem area work together, we cofounded MIT Collaborative Initiatives (MIT-CI).
>
> We are interested in speeding up the pace of innovation and change in all areas of societal concern, including health-medical issues. The mission of MIT-CI comes from an

understanding that there is power in acknowledging and learning from any successful transformation, whether in our own silo of expertise or someone else's.

Over the past seven years, MIT-CI has brought leaders from multiple areas of expertise together for highly interactive meetings focused on knowledge sharing and idea creation. Attendees at these meetings have ranged from the Secretary for Veterans Affairs and Chairman of the Joint Chiefs of Staff, to the CEOs of Stonyfield Farms, Coca-Cola, and the Mayo Clinic, the president of Doctors Without Borders, MIT institute professors, and other leaders in healthcare, research, business, academia, NGOs, and the military.

From these meetings we have developed projects that apply the same interdisciplinary approach combined with systems thinking to significant, intractable problems that resist easy fixes: stroke, childhood obesity, and posttraumatic stress in the active military. On each of these projects MIT-CI has worked with an academic research partner with expertise in systems thinking and design.

The potential value of our approach, which considers a broad range of factors affecting an issue and then determines where the pivotal intersections occur, is great.

MIT-CI has partnered with principal investigators from the Harvard Graduate School of Design, the Urban Design Lab in the Earth Institute at Columbia University, and the MIT Sociotechnical Systems Research Center, and has built multidisciplinary advisory boards to guide, inform, and promote these research efforts.

Each of these efforts has led to innovative solutions:

- In *Stroke*, an area that was generally seen to be working well by the medical community at the time, the project challenged the standard protocol and demonstrated key areas where changes in the system could save money and improve outcomes.
- The *Childhood Obesity* project determined that lots of good work was being done to fight this epidemic but that unless

there was a change in the food system—the way food is produced, processed, and distributed—these efforts were fighting an uphill battle. The project is now working on developing a tool that will demonstrate the health impact of every dollar spent on infrastructure to support regional food systems.

- As of this date, the *Posttraumatic Stress* project is still underway.

In 2011, facing the reality that many of the societal issues that were seen to have reached an impasse when MIT Collaborative Initiatives was formed were still challenging leadership and the economy, we held two meetings focused on *log jams*. The meetings provided a forum for discussion and debate on the value of systems thinking and collaboration in breaking through log jams of ideology and conflicting incentives to effective action. They highlighted MIT-CI's experience as well as models of successful application and difficulties of this approach in business, government, the U.S. military, and healthcare.

A fundamental outcome of these meetings was the realization that to break a log jam you need innovative leadership, cross-specialty collaboration, a way to measure success, and an acceptance of the possibility of failure. Also clear was consensus that rising leaders must be included in the conversation if we expect future innovation and a shift in the paradigm of solution building.

In response to these findings, MIT-CI is currently launching the Albright Challenge, using what we have learned in the past seven years to challenge rising leaders to come together around an issue of societal concern. The focus of the Challenge will be an intense five-day working session based at MIT. In that session our leaders will be put into teams of ten to twelve people and given a specific challenge to work through. The sessions will be facilitated using design methodology uniquely suited to managing complex problems and promoting idea generation. The teams will also be given an opportunity to work with some of the most powerful leaders of our time in small group or lecture settings.

Based on the Helsinki Design Lab's Studio Model for driving systemic change, the goals of the Albright Challenge are to generate creative solutions to seemingly intractable problems; spark action and build momentum towards real change; develop a pool of leaders open to cross-disciplinary collaboration, design methodology, and fostering innovation; provide a dynamic environment for rising leaders and current leaders to interact and learn from each other; and create a community where our participants can "act their way into new thinking."

Connect—Concrete Steps for Putting This Discipline into Action

Individual

Establishing relationships and connections should be a part of everyone's everyday habit. It's as important as everything else we do on the job. They should never be sacrificed in the effort to make some particular task happen—by ignoring people in our haste, or humiliating them when we catch them in a mistake, or the hundred other ways we can hurt people as we try to get a job done. In the end, those relationships and those people are what matter for the bigger picture, the big results we are looking for from our team—not to mention the positive effect on our lives and health when we work in harmony with others.

When focusing too narrowly on getting the task at hand completed—an issue of the moment—endangers a long-term relationship, we have to step back and restore our priorities. And while connections will occasionally be weakened by the stress associated with projects of great importance and the natural pressures of change, we should always take the high road of maintaining strong connection, rather than the low road of conflict.

Team and Organization

In addition to making personal connections, an innovation leader has to make sure that team members connect with one another, with the company at large, and with the world outside. The team leader can help develop internal connections by ensuring that team members understand the requirements of each corporate stakeholder, so that everyone can work together to reach the overall objectives, not just their individual pieces of the puzzle. Team and organizational leaders can help forge external connections by encouraging participation in industry events; ensuring close customer contact; and bringing in speakers, industry experts, partners, vendors, and others who can widen staff horizons.

We can also reexamine the prevailing system of rewards. Do incentives exist for team leaders to form working relationships with other teams? How about between business units? Can bonus systems be set up that reward, for example, sales growth throughout the organization rather than just in our own small groups? Finally we must encourage an evaluation of values and character in the criteria for recruiting new employees. Many companies are already doing this.

How to Connect
- ✓ Connect globally, broadly across industries, institutions, organizations, and age groups
- ✓ Connect with strategy, systems, and processes, as well as with people
- ✓ Connect when you don't need a favor from people
- ✓ Connect strategically, not focused on immediate needs or transactions
- ✓ Connect openly, encouraging mutual trust and integrity
- ✓ Connect constantly, seizing every moment and every opportunity
- ✓ Connect with empathy—treat everyone as they personally wish to be treated

(continued)

✓ Connect generously—do not be calculating constantly

✓ Connect is *not* taking advantage of people or using them for your benefit

✓ Help to connect other people together for their mutual benefit

✓ Help other people whenever you can, not only for your own immediate interests

✓ Connections require time-consuming efforts, so be patient

✓ Successful connections demand emotional intelligence on both sides

承

Chapter 6

Commit

The eight disciplines I describe in this book are closely inter-related. Each one supports the others, and there is a certain degree of overlap among them. This is probably more so for *Commit* than for any other single discipline. *Commit* is where the "rubber meets the road" for innovation. If the other disciplines we have discussed so far are missing in our work, the result is usually a lack of commitment. When these others disciplines are in place, however, our intentions can turn into action. Because of the disciplines' strong interdependencies, this chapter returns to many of the key principles discussed so far, while providing additional detail and perspective.

Commit 承 *Cheng*

Cheng is an ancient word, used to mean "by order of" or "in the name of." The term 承諾 *chengnuo*, created by adding 諾 *nuo*, means not only "to take on," but also to "agree to do so verbally." The left side of the character 諾 *nuo* is 言 *yen*, meaning "say" or "indicate."

"To commit" in English means "to agree to be bound to a certain course of action," or "to pledge."

Good leaders commit themselves to tasks or missions as if their lives depended on it. Once that commitment is made, they must believe in it wholeheartedly, and take action to fulfill that commitment.

Footnote: Even an Emperor in China takes his order from "Heavenly forces." In traditional Chinese terminology the Son of Heaven, or the Emperor, must receive the "mandate" of Heaven, bestowed on him from above and supported by the people.

Culture and Commitment

An open and inspiring environment that encourages risk-taking is the ground on which a successful innovation culture is built. A shared vision and sense of purpose provides the framework for motivating and aligning employee ingenuity.

Tarkan Maner, previous CEO of Wyse Technology, serial entrepreneur, and investor, finds inspiration in history and a rallying cry to motivate his team when obstacles must be overcome:

One of my favorite mottos is a quote from Hannibal: "There is always a way! We will find the way! If there is no way, we will build the way!" I use that quote a lot with my team, because you face difficult challenges when you are innovating. Challenges are guaranteed, so you need to be resilient. You can't give up. You can learn, you can adapt, but don't quit.

Keep working on it because there is always a way. Passion creates persistence and persistence creates success.

Appropriate incentives, guidelines, and processes manage the downside of risk-taking without continuing to foster a fear of failure. Admiral Mullen has some sage advice for leaders based on his own experience with failure and risk and how they relate to commitment. He asserts that we must learn how to fail constructively. The personal failure he refers to happened after he took his first command and crashed a gasoline tanker into a buoy. The event nearly cost then-Lt. Mullen his career.

I think for an organization to keep remaking itself for the future, there has to be some high risk. . . . In my own life, one of the reasons that I am so tolerant of failure is because I failed very early. It's less about the failure than it was: What did I do after I failed? How did I pick myself up? What did I learn from that? And how did I incorporate the learnings into future steps?

There are risks that leaders take associated with investments, with people, with careers, and with success and failure. . . .

If leaders take that risk, then the organization will as well.

But if a leader just runs an organization at status quo, it will just keep generating the same kind of relatively weak outcomes certainly with respect to innovation. . . . I think you have to use risk mitigation in any new area, where there may not be a lot of data, certainly not much experience or much history. That can be very difficult, but you have to try to learn that in a new area, feed-back your lessons almost in real time as you continue to move forward, continue to innovate.

Dean Kamen draws a wonderful analogy between the kind of support he received from his parents for his youthful adventures and the kind of culture corporations need to create where failure is allowed.

My parents ran the family in the same way I run DEKA. Which is, yes, they wanted us to get a good education, they wanted us to learn all the tools, but if I wanted to try something new and different, they encouraged us.

If I or my brother or somebody tried to do something really different and failed, you know they were disappointed, but they didn't ridicule us, they supported us. They helped us even when—like all good parents—they were trying to protect their kids from failure. They would urge us to do something more conventional, but in the end if I said "No, I really want to try this," even though they were nervous and even though they were protective parents like big corporate management people might try to protect their status quo, in the end my mother and my father always said, "Oh whatever you are going to do, we are going to support you." And they did.

It was enormously valuable to me that I knew that, even if I failed, I could get up and try again, and they would be there supporting me. It's sort of what I am suggesting companies ought to do. They ought to try to avoid the same mistakes of the past, they ought to rely on education and knowledge and experience, BUT at some point they ought to say, "All right, you really want to try something different? We know it's high risk; we know you will probably have to do a bunch of things that won't work. We can tolerate that; we can overcome it, and we can keep going."

If corporate management was as supportive and indulgent of our passion inside a company as my parents were inside a family, I think those corporations would, in the end, have greater rate of innovation than they do now by plodding along, being conventional, avoiding risk.

You know—the safest place for a ship is in the harbor. But it just doesn't do any good there. I think companies need to take reasonable risks and support people, even when they are having troubles in what they are trying to do. That's what my parents did.

As discussed in Chapter 2, *Lead*, in many corporate cultures, failure of any type has negative consequences. Not all failures result in lost jobs or denied promotion opportunities. However, they almost always result in a loss of organizational standing and credibility. This does more than simply demoralize the individuals involved and make it more difficult for them to gain support for future efforts. For the organization as a whole, it reinforces the negative consequences of trying to do things differently and better.

Tom Mendoza describes the antidote to this as something he calls a *culture of safety*.

> Many of the true innovations at NetApp actually happened at a very low level in the company. There's a culture of safety here in the sense that we understand not all ideas are going to make sense and you have to be somewhat vulnerable to come forward with your idea; therefore the culture has to say it is okay to be wrong. If you never can be wrong, you can't have innovation; it's impossible. I think it is very, very important that if someone pursues an idea with passion and integrity and gets the most out of it given the circumstances, then you do what you need to do to make sure they don't get killed. Even if the task's not done, if they significantly move the ball forward, you make sure something good happens to them. Then you can ask, okay, who's going to step up next?

I think Tom has hit on a critically important requirement for an innovation culture, and it is one that I don't always see practiced. I actually had the very great fortune of attending one of the last training classes delivered by W. Edwards Deming, the great management thinker, whose insights and observations are still relevant and useful today. Dr. Deming called upon leaders to "drive out fear," and observed that it is more likely to be faulty processes, rather than people, responsible for most mistakes. Tom has applied very similar thinking to getting the very best from employees. He recognizes that it's unreasonable to expect people to behave in ways that are counter to their interests. He doesn't demand that they "step out of their safety zone." He widens that zone.

Innovation Management in the Safety Zone

Leaders of teams and organizations can widen safety zones for their employees by clearly differentiating the criteria for "acceptable failures"—what Dean Kamen calls "kissing frogs"—and carefully contrasting these from the type of failures that put the larger enterprise at risk. When I led State Street's Office of Innovation under Jim Phalen, he illustrated the point succinctly and humorously to a global audience of State Street employees, saying "Don't get me wrong, this commitment to innovation doesn't mean we're looking for highly creative trading practices!"

Clear guidelines allow employees to take calculated risks in a way that serves the interests of the organization and its goals. When people understand the limits within which they can experiment, when they know that they won't be penalized for doing so, and when they can see potential for achievement and reward, employees have no reason not to invest their ingenuity. Appropriate innovation management practices provide the support as well as the controls needed to oversee and optimize these efforts.

Most organizational controls seek to maximize conformity and predictability. Frequently, people who have spent much of their careers managing these controls and the related processes don't even recognize how inconsistent these principles are with the requirements of an innovation culture. This is why folding innovation projects into existing practices, such as program management functions, often creates issues.

The goal of most projects in a corporate setting is to deliver the expected results on time and on budget. The goal of an innovation project, on the other hand, is to assess and harvest new ways of creating business value.

Projects of all types, innovation projects included, certainly need to meet or manage expectations regarding budget, resources, and schedule. However, traditional program management practices often assume an ability to define timing and allocate funding in advance.

They then monitor the extent to which projects meet these commitments. There's also an assumption that, barring unforeseen calamity, each project will continue to move forward. This leads to a failure-avoidance mentality as well as a focus on requirements such as compliance that might have no relevance for experimental projects.

Effective innovation management practices are built around an entirely different life cycle and portfolio management model. The assumptions are much more "Darwinian" in that only a select number of funded projects is expected to move forward after each round of funding. Projects that don't move forward can still add tremendous value to the organization by virtue of having tested assumptions and delivered lessons learned. The commitment is to maximize organizational learning and growth rather than meet preset project delivery expectations.

The IBM Way

I asked Linda Sanford, senior vice president of enterprise transformation at IBM, how IBM perceives and manages for potential failure when pursuing innovative ideas or new businesses. Here's her response:

> Like any successful organization, IBM is organized and managed to drive execution and results. However, we also realize that we need to have an explicit management system in place that is focused on innovation, testing new ideas and new businesses. Within this part of the management system, you have to plan for some failure, because if you don't, it probably means you are not pushing the envelope enough.
>
> IBM has made significant progress in changing the way it manages new, emerging businesses, and it has deployed a range of approaches to support this. A good example is the program called Emerging Business Opportunities, or EBOs, a structured program that helps identify, fund, and shepherd new businesses from ideation through growth.
>
> Once a business opportunity is selected as an EBO, we give it special care and feeding, including A-team leadership,

sponsorship by a senior vice president, protected funding, and strategic milestones that are measured differently than existing businesses.

The EBO process produced some outstanding success stories, including our Linux and life sciences businesses. But not everything was a home run. There were some ideas that didn't get off the ground. The key is we didn't punish the leaders and the teams involved in EBOs that didn't pan out.

We've learned that you take a risk, you learn from it, and these leaders benefit from that experience. You can't be a company that makes markets, a progressive organization viewed as an innovation leader, unless you are willing to risk some missteps. Setbacks and failures are a necessary part of innovation . . . you just want to manage them in a controlled way.

Funding as Commitment

Establishing funding for the kinds of efforts we are discussing here is in itself an important and highly visible commitment to innovation. It provides an important signal to the organization that top management is serious about innovation. Normally, when departments experience budgetary challenges, their innovation projects are often the first expenses to disappear. This is why an enduring commitment to innovation from the top is critical for organizations to continuously progress toward improvement. One very effective and visible way to do this is to separate innovation funding from the general operating budget. Depending on organizational culture and preferences, centralized and/ or decentralized management processes are implemented to assess innovation project business cases, oversee funding, and define the governance model for executing and evaluating projects. After a proof-of-concept or pilot, the innovation project can then be moved out of the innovation program and be funded and managed using more traditional processes.

For companies, the critical factor in managing innovation projects is the concept of *early failure*, so that the reasonable but ultimately unsuccessful attempts at innovation do no irreparable harm to the company and at the same time make learning possible. One way to do this is through vigorously testing assumptions up front. These can be assumptions regarding customer or market interest, competitive positioning, costs to develop and produce, technology readiness, and more. I'll speak more about this in Chapter 7, *Execute*, but for the *Commit* discipline it's important to note now that, over the course of an innovation initiative, various opportunities to test the idea's viability will occur. Taking advantage of those opportunities will provide multiple points of validation throughout the process, and will either confirm the initiative's continued viability or alert project sponsors that the time has come to focus attention and resources elsewhere.

This is true in the nonprofit world, too. Gerald Chertavian, founder of Year Up, puts it this way:

> I think companies signed on to Year Up's intern program with the intention to help their community and did not recognize we could help them with a challenge they are facing. But what we knew, and they found, is that not only is it good for the companies, but they can start using Year Up as a talent pipeline, and this is very different from doing it because it happens to be a nice, charitable act.

Although Year Up first gained traction from the charitable aspect of the program, with minimal funding, their commitment to corporate citizenship grew into a clear economic benefit as well for the company. Gerald continues:

> In fact, in the model pitch, we discourage people from doing this as a charitable act. Instead we price it in a way that forces someone to ask *is this valuable?* And the proof of that is that we typically get money from the company's line functions, rather than the corporate foundation, and the line person doesn't have money to waste. They won't do something that isn't in the company's interest, even though they see that it's good for the community, which is another benefit. I think the corporations are also beginning to see this as a way to increase

employee satisfaction and company morale. It's been demonstrated that people working with interns are actually happier with their companies.

At first tiptoeing into the program, companies then had an opportunity to observe and measure its continued viability, and then began to embrace it more fully. In some cases, the results of these observations may not be definitive, but there may still be value in sight. So it continues. The initiative needs to come to a *quick* end, however, if we learn that our key assumptions were wrong, or that the economics to support continuing our efforts just aren't there. It's also possible that, while everything is going exactly as planned, another way to achieve the goal—better, faster, or less expensive—comes along and we see the need to change course.

Nathan Myhrvold has seen countless ideas come to fruition and also many that never made it. He believes that the question of whether to stay the course with a project or give up on it is one of the most difficult to answer:

> Probably the hardest thing in technology is to know when you should keep pushing on a project—because maybe in the next version or the next turn of the crank or in a year, it will take off—versus when do you give up. I don't think there is any perfect way to do that. It's a question venture capitalists struggle with, entrepreneurs, people in companies. You have to make the best judgment you can relative to understanding what's out there in the market and why you got into this thing in the first place.
>
> A common mistake, for example, is that when people get into a project, their initial hypothesis about the market or about the product is wrong. Oops, it isn't successful, nobody wants it, or nobody is willing to pay for it or whatever. That's a really good time to step back and say, maybe we should quit. But a lot of people don't because they are embarrassed and say, well, maybe we can *pivot*—that's the trendy term—we are going to pivot.

When a young entrepreneur told me he was going to pivot, I said, "You mean you are totally wrong and you are now going to change your mind?" And the entrepreneur laughed and said, "Well, yeah, but these days we call that pivoting." Well, that's fine, but you have to make sure that what you are going to do next is something that still makes sense.

There is a strong human desire and a human need to say, "I am so far into this, I am not going to quit now." And so you wind up talking yourself into something that might still kind of make sense because of X, Y, and Z. Well that's a tricky thing to do, because you can fool yourself for a long period of time and dig a very deep hole.

I was recently talking to an entrepreneur. He had a cool idea, raised the money, got the people. Oops, the idea doesn't work. Well, they then had this clever idea and said "Well, hey—what is our current thing useful for?" They found a second application. It's too early for me to tell, if that was a really smart idea or a dumb idea. So I asked the entrepreneur, and he said, "You know, it's great because we could use all of the stuff that we already did." And I said, "Yes, but would you have started that way to begin with, or are you just afraid of admitting that you screwed up the first time and you should actually go do something better?" He said, "Well, I hadn't thought of it that way, I will think about it."

And since this is a young, proud, wonderful guy, he is probably going to convince himself, that, "Oh yes, it still makes perfect, perfect sense." But my guess is that it doesn't make any sense, and that if he was trying to do this up front, he would say, "I am not going to go in that market at all." So I think he's probably kind of pushing it because he is too proud to admit that he should quit. And to a point, that's okay.

The reason I say that is because you don't want quitters. You don't want people who are going to fold at the first sign of adversity, because almost every new idea has carried some adversity. The new, innovative idea that is suddenly welcomed with open arms by everybody is extremely rare. So rare that it almost doesn't exist. So, you want some perseverance.

And the whole question then is to ask, when do you keep going for it? When do you say, "It's going to motivate the team, they want to be successful, they had a setback, and the investment is long gone" versus saying, "We just think this is hopeless"? And again, I don't have any simple way to do that. You just have to make a decision for yourself, trying to be intellectually honest, that you ask yourself, "Is this really worth doing? Does my thesis still make sense? If I'm starting from scratch, right now, would I go do this?" And if the answer is that if you were starting from scratch you'd never do this, but you're doing it now because you're kind of stuck, then I'd say, "Really? Shouldn't you rethink this?"

Dean Kamen gave me an interesting answer when I asked him how we can recognize ideas that will ultimately create business value:

You can't.

You have to begin by accepting failure. Most people hear only about the successes. The failures are far more frequent, but can be considered part of the process of innovation if they come to a quick end *once there is no value in sight*. But the process that produces more failures than successes still has to be encouraged in order to eventually discover new strategic value.

Dean's words, then, confirm the need for unproductive efforts to be quickly redirected, and when there is clearly no prospective opportunity for adding value. Another aspect we should mention here regarding Dean's comment on failure as part of the process is that failure should be regarded as an important part of learning. People need to be comfortable openly discussing what failed and why, so they and others can learn. It's important, then, for our organizational culture to encourage us to acknowledge our failures, rather than cover them up.

Effective innovation management processes define approaches to manage risk, develop and assess proposals and business cases, allocate funding, test assumptions, deliver business value (whether through project success or learning), and reward the right behavior as well the right results.

Tarkan Maner provides another perspective on decision-making and commitment. It is a lesson he learned as young man at a crossroads in his life. At the time, he had to decide between two very different options, and he knew that either choice would dramatically impact his future direction. He was struggling greatly with this important decision and asked an older, trusted advisor for advice on which was the better path:

> I'll never forget what he said, and I have heeded his advice ever since. First, he pointed out that both paths had integrity and were not as different as they appeared. Then he told me that the real question is not which path to choose. It is a question of ensuring that whatever path I take, I make that the right path. I learned that the one you choose doesn't matter. You just work tirelessly to make your decision the right one.

Personal and Team Commitment

Legend has it that the Spanish conquistador Hernando Cortes ensured the commitment of his troops by destroying the ships on which they had sailed to the new world, thus preventing his crew from escape or retreat. There is a similar story from ancient Chinese history about a rebellion against the Qin dynasty in which the leader sunk the boats and burned all but three days of rations in order to motivate the army in their fight against overwhelming odds. While these examples are not very effective risk management practices and certainly not recommended motivation techniques anymore, they have led to the concept of *burning the boats*: taking action that demonstrates your commitment.

In 2009, for example, State Street Corporation issued a press release announcing its commitment to saving $575 to $625 million over the next five years. It takes strong leadership to undertake such bold and decisive action. This public commitment energized the entire company. Our top leadership team and every employee took on the challenge, bonding together to achieve that commitment.

Innovation leaders must, in some similar way, commit themselves if they expect the company to come together, commit to, and accomplish major goals. As Admiral Mullen indicated earlier, leaders must be the first to take the risk.

Early in my career at State Street, I took that risk. At the time, we were using a network that did not have a continuously available architecture and was challenging to expand and manage. Although it served our business needs at that time, I knew that network availability and resiliency could be improved and disruptions minimized.

I became an advocate for migrating to a new virtual network technology that some believed had not sufficiently matured for most large corporations to implement companywide and/or globally. Several members of my own team didn't support the idea, either. There were risks, and anything less than complete success could have vast negative consequences.

Executives from corporate support functional areas assembled in a conference room to discuss the business case. After reviewing a report prepared by an outside consulting firm, the group agreed with its findings that the capital investment would be excessive, the return-on-investment insufficient, and the risk far too great. All the executives—except for me—concluded that there was no compelling case for us to move forward with the project.

I was not persuaded. I didn't think the study's numbers were correct, but I didn't argue with the group or express anger about their decision. Like Tarkan Maner and Hannibal, I believe that, "There is always a way! We will find the way! If there is no way, we will build the way!" So, I left the room quietly, and in everyone's mind—except mine—the issue was closed.

After leaving the conference room, I went straight to see my boss, Joe Antonellis, State Street's CIO. I knocked on his door and walked in, and started asking some pointed questions.

"Joe, who would you call if there was any network issue?"

He pointed at me and said, "You!"

So, I asked him, "If I am the one you would call, then shouldn't I be the one to make this strategic network decision?" Before he responded, I asked again, "Why should this decision be made by people who are not responsible for the network and are not the ones you would call?"

Joe looked at me and said that the team thought the risk and impact of redoing the entire network was too big. Evidently someone had already spoken with him. I responded that their concerns were certainly justified, but there were ways to mitigate the risk. I explained that my goal was to build a continuously available network with a generous capacity for growth. I asked Joe to allow me to do a study with my team to see if we could do the job and save the company money.

Joe asked me how much time I would need to complete the study. I thought for a few seconds and answered, "About 90 days." Then I added, "I'll *bet* we can find a way to save three times more than the consulting firm's study projected in our annual expenses."

He then asked me, "If I approve the study, will you guarantee that you'll find that amount of savings?"

I said, "No, I can't guarantee it, but I'm pretty certain."

Joe laughed and jokingly complained, "Well, if you want to bet, you've got to bet *something*!"

I thought fast and responded, "Okay. I bet my job. If my study can't find three times the consulting firm's projected savings, you can fire me."

Joe grinned and told me he liked the bet. He flipped his calendar forward 90 days and wrote, "Madge bet her job if she doesn't deliver the savings she committed in the 90-day study."

We both liked the bet, so we laughed and shook hands on it.

I needed to assign someone to lead the study who would be objective and credible. I asked one of my direct report managers, who was not the overall network manager, but rather managed the service delivery function for one business unit, to lead the study. He would be working with a worldwide team including members from finance, procurement, our network engineers, and representatives of many related functions worldwide.

The team got to work immediately. With the 90-day deadline approaching, my team had not come back to show me their business case yet. I began to worry that I might not be able to deliver the study in time. And I began to wonder if maybe the amount of savings I had committed to wasn't there. *Would Joe really fire me?* I wondered.

When I asked the team leader what was holding up the study, he said, "I'm having some problems with the projected savings." Then I really began to worry.

"You can't find the savings?" I asked.

He smiled. "It's not that—the savings number is *way too large.* I think there must be mistakes in our calculations. I have asked the team to check all the numbers again."

Now I got excited and asked him to review it with me immediately. We got the entire team together with finance, procurement, and the engineers to review the business case. We went through the numbers together in detail and made a few corrections. When we finished, we were showing our expense savings to be *nine times* what the consulting firm had projected! Needless to say, I was relieved, and the entire team was absolutely thrilled with our results. We knew we were ready to present our business case to my boss, Joe Antonellis.

The scheduled meeting day finally arrived. The team was really excited, but we tried to keep straight faces, not wanting to tip Joe off. I asked the project leader to review the overall study, and asked our finance person to review all the business case numbers. At the end of our presentation, Joe expressed his surprise and pleasure with the results. He told us to prepare to present them to Ron Logue, our CEO. We did, and Ron's response was also very positive. He accepted our business case and approved the project immediately.

When we finished the project, the yearly savings were twelve times greater than the consulting firm projected and more than four times greater than what I committed to in my bet with Joe. Our new network technology allowed us to develop all kinds of new capabilities; provided better network resiliency, availability, and capacity; and positioned us for meeting the requirements of accelerated business growth worldwide.

And I kept my job!

Timing and Commitment

I have always been fascinated by the concept of a self-fulfilling prophecy, in which the beliefs that people hold about the future are what actually bring that future into existence. I think this concept holds particularly true for innovation. If we have confidence and are ready to commit ourselves to overcoming challenges, viewing them merely as tasks on the path to success, we will succeed. With this kind of approach and mind-set, effective team members keep each other focused on the goal and what can be gained, and they do not retreat when the going gets tough.

In traditional Western marriage ceremonies, anyone who could show why the couple should not be lawfully wed was asked to "speak now, or forever hold your peace." In the same way, the practice of inviting fact-based objections and concerns before commitments are made should be built into standard processes—and into the culture itself. People can only commit when they know they have been heard and their input has been thoughtfully considered. Of course, if we try to address every concern or requirement in advance, we risk becoming paralyzed. On the other hand, if we are dismissive of others, commitment will be impossible to achieve. Leaders must keep a delicate balance, listening closely and respectfully to what people are saying. Significant concerns don't need to stop progress. They can often be translated into "risks" and actively managed on an ongoing basis. True commitment comes once collaborators understand each other's requirements, interests, concerns, and the capabilities of their constituents—and develop plans that reflect them.

Once the strategy and plans are in place, leaders have the right to expect every team member's support and commitment. Suggestions can still be made along the way, and legitimate concerns addressed whenever they arise. But committed team members will take ownership of the problems they encounter and do their best to solve them.

The following graphic shows one of my mother's favorite sayings, "Resolve the problem before others make it worse," and it still comes to mind whenever I see that it's time to commit to early action, before positions become unshakable and momentum shifts.

Resolve the problem before others make it worse
先 xiān 發 fā 制 zhì 人 rén

The issue of timing is critical where committing to innovation is concerned. If we attempt to commit too early—or inspire others to commit too early—we may be disappointed if the pieces of the puzzle are not yet ready to be assembled. On the other hand, if we move to commit too late, the path we are trying to take may already be so crowded that we won't be able to make any headway, maintain a course, or have our voice heard above the crowd.

Preparing ourselves and our team to commit at the right time also depends on positioning the initiative within the organization's overall strategy, and, when necessary, presenting the business case at just the right time. The appropriate executive or executive committee in the organization, after all, will have to commit to funding and staffing the innovation, and presenting our case too early or too late in the budget cycle or without taking other initiatives into consideration will greatly reduce our chances of success.

Effective leaders know how to lead by example, to engage others, to encourage them to commit. But, as important as it is to commit to a path, commitment shouldn't be confused with inflexibility. In fact, the two are incompatible. Leaders and their teams must be both committed and flexible about new ideas, new learning, and changes along the way.

Let's now turn to our levels of effectiveness we associated with the discipline of commit, and let's frame it in the context of risk.

Commit: Levels of Effectiveness

Level One: Avoids Risk

At Level One we are overly cautious about risking change in order to avoid "egg-on-the-face" issues. We don't differentiate between personal risk and business risk—it's all personal. Typically we add to—but do not change—as a way of hedging bets. We are unlikely to persevere in the face of great difficulty or impending "failure."

Level Two: Minimizes Risk

At Level Two we are willing to take a stand about what needs to change, and we set about changing it. But we are focused on minimizing risk rather than managing it. We recognize the roller-coaster life cycle of innovation projects and do not bail out when the going gets tough. We soldier through when obstacles appear—we don't retreat. We are decisive and accountable.

Level Three: Manages Risk

At Level Three we know how to manage business and financial risk, leveraging experimentation, fast-failure, and other strategies that significantly reduce it. Our risks are *calculated*, not avoided. We put ourselves on the line, carrying personal risk in a way that inspires others and makes others feel safe. We anticipate difficulties, and we under-commit while always trying to over-deliver.

Commit—Concrete Steps for Putting This Discipline into Action

Individual

As innovators, we commit to change by putting ourselves on the line. In effect, we have to stand up and say, "I think we can do this better, and this is the way I'd like to try." We don't have to bet our job or career every time we propose a new initiative, but we do have to make it clear that we're willing to take a calculated risk. Then we can better engage the support and commitment of our organization and the team on which we will rely.

Team and Organization

Teams and organizations commit to innovation by providing employees with a culture of safety that welcomes ideas and recognizes that not all of these ideas will pan out. This requires a shift in the processes, controls, and other cultural signals that shape behavior. Teams and organizations must recognize the types of results that their current practices reward and the types of failures that are penalized. Then they can redefine them to better support a culture of innovation. By changing these cultural signals and implementing clear guidelines and practices for managing innovation risks, funding, projects, and learning, teams and organizations demonstrate their own commitment to innovation.

How to Commit

✓ Passion creates commitment and persistence

✓ Commit wholeheartedly to the path you choose

✓ Commit wisely, with carefully calculated risks

✓ Commit and obtain buy-in from your team and organization

✓ Commit funding, staffing, resources, support, P&L, and so forth

✓ Commit delivery of functions and features, and on a reasonable schedule

✓ Commit, but remember that it's better to under-promise and over-deliver than it is to over-promise

✓ Commit, but maintain an open mind. Always allow people to discuss issues and ideas

✓ Commit, but be flexible. Be aware of changes and unexpected events or incidents, which might require further consideration

✓ Commitment is not dictatorship

行

Chapter 7

Execute

There is a Japanese proverb that addresses the issue of action or, as we would put it today, *Execution*: "A vision without action is a daydream. Action without vision is a nightmare."

We all know imaginative people who have great ideas about how things should be and a solid understanding of how things actually are. Since they know the starting line as well as the finish, they are able to clearly mark the surest route. Yet we also know people who tend to focus only on one or the other. They are more likely to get lost along the route. Those with a meaningful vision for the future can move the organization very far ahead. Those with a realistic understanding of the present rarely struggle as they line others up for the journey.

When I asked John Thompson, the very successful former executive at IBM, former chairman, CEO, and president of Symantec, and now CEO of Virtual Instruments, what advice he would give aspiring innovators, he expressed a sentiment very similar to this Japanese proverb. He told me that he would recommend first that they never stop dreaming. Then, he said he would tell them, "Innovation is about dreams, but don't ever assume that just because you have great dreams, they will happen automatically. You have got to be focused on the execution part, too. People who dream big and execute well are the most successful people in this industry, no question about it."

Effective innovators know that they—or their teams—need the right mix of skills to both envision and achieve. They also recognize the essential elements of effective execution—quality and timeliness. And they know that they must balance them without compromising either.

Execute 行 *Xing*

In Chinese, the character 行 *xing*, second tone, used for both the verb "to do" or "to step," and the noun "action," is an ideal ideograph for *execute*. On the left side of the character is the radical for two people or "to step," on the right 丁 indicating reverse, in other words, "in motion." There are many compound phrases built on *xing*, such as 執行, *zhixing*, meaning "to take charge," or 進行 *jinxing*, meaning "to be in motion to pursue a course of action." Both of these terms can be used to express more specific actions related to the execution of business plans and the necessary division of labor, and as I have done in earlier pages, I will introduce a few more of them later in this chapter.

Footnote: An ideograph is a visual representation of something. My Chinese given name is the same character, 行 *xing*. My father used the Cantonese spelling *heng*, instead of the Mandarin *xing*, clearly hoping that I would be a decisive child—that is, one who "executed" many plans.

Meeting the Highest Standard for Our Astronauts

I started my career as a scientific programmer with IBM. At that time, IBM had a contract with NASA for technological support and software development. I had the great good fortune to be assigned to work on software for NASA's last three Gemini spaceflights. My husband Werner and I met and worked on this same project. As a young programmer, it was an incredible honor and challenge to contribute to such a critical mission. I realized how important this assignment was when I started working with the project manager who trained all the astronauts. He told me about the horrible things that could happen if there were errors in our software products. Not only could errors damage our country's reputation worldwide, they might even cause the death of our astronauts. This responsibility frightened and motivated me.

I became relentless about having zero defects in my programming. My assignment was to develop onboard computer code for the Gemini flights, and my husband's assignment was to develop the mainframe computer programs for ground simulation of those same flights. Our mathematical calculations required fifteen-digit decimal point accuracy, with absolutely zero tolerance of any errors. My program and my husband's program both had to produce the very same results—all fifteen-digit decimal points.

The very high standards and self-discipline we had to embrace made us much better programmers. We were determined to deliver our software programs flawlessly. This entire experience taught me why a zero-defects standard was so important and that we could ultimately achieve it. The impact on all stakeholder reputations and the potential cost in lives and money from defects in any of the spaceflights would be insurmountable. So, I worked around the clock to make certain that my software was delivered ahead of schedule and with zero defects. Because of my early training, I steadfastly maintained the same discipline, applying it in all my work throughout my career.

Flawless Execution

The notion of acceptable fast failure that we discussed in prior chapters is sometimes misinterpreted. I have seen teams mistakenly apply it to the way they approach their projects, believing that an innovative mind-set is somehow at odds with a focus on quality. I don't mean these teams *knowingly* introduced quality issues just to get the job done faster or more cheaply. However, they dismissed concerns and even ideas about improving execution quality, believing that innovation required a willingness to "let the chips fall where they may." In other words, the team wanted to break away from the cultural legacy of risk aversion that normally slows progress. Yet they did so in a way that lowered quality standards and led to mediocre execution. This is not the same as "embracing failure." When we make predictable mistakes, we waste time and resources. We also lose support and credibility. Failure is acceptable when it allows us to learn something new, not when it happens because we are ignoring the lessons of the past. Acceptable failure is a matter of *raising our sights*, not *lowering our standards*.

Many people don't think of flawless execution as an achievable outcome. In fact, it isn't always achievable. But it should always be our goal and our aspiration. At the same time, however, we must also be true to the *cost and benefits of a business case* as our guiding principle. Sometimes it is a judgment call regarding the cost of the error to the business versus the cost of zero defects. If we are traveling on a plane, we definitely want zero defects. We don't want to be the passenger of an airline that settles for a Six Sigma defect rate.

By simply striving for that ultimate ideal, we sometimes reach it. And when we don't, we can reflect on why and learn something new. A commitment to flawless execution makes us good today and even better tomorrow.

Flawless execution applies to projects, to operations, to any activity in any kind of business. And in some, as Ming Tsai points out, flaws in execution are very visible and immediately apparent to all. On the other hand, when it's all going right, that's immediately apparent as well, with one of the rewards being a rush of instant gratification:

> I will know tonight, each night, how good we are. I heard yesterday that we're a great restaurant—from customers, from reviews, from wherever. Today we don't know yet—we haven't served one dinner. And so we have an opportunity. It's like Broadway. We always say that in the business: It's showtime! When the lights go up: It's showtime! You've got to put on

that happy face, you have to excel, give great service and make great food, season it well, cook it perfectly. It's live. That's the best part of being a chef—it is live. It's Broadway. If you fall or mess up or forget a line it's obvious. The same goes for the kitchen. If you over-cook, under-cook, over-season, or under-season, if you spill wine—whatever it might be—it's obvious. But when it works, it is instant gratification. Your head is on the block every day and when you do excel, and it does work well and your machine is oiled and running smoothly, there is not a better feeling in the world!

It's important to point out that by flawless execution I don't mean "zero errors," but rather "zero negative impact" to the customers and business. That is, ensuring that mistakes do not cause disruptions. In the world of IT infrastructure, for instance, we can architect solutions to have continuous availability. This design recognizes the inevitability of issues such as hardware failure and builds in compensatory mechanisms that immediately take over to avoid service interruption. We can apply the same principles and planning to projects. For example, we always had very thorough alternate recovery plans in case our execution failed. Sometimes half of our plan was devoted to preparing for the possibility of rollback and recovery.

Several years ago, my State Street team introduced our 21st Century Technology Infrastructure solution in Europe. It was a multiyear project that involved establishing a regional data center in a new office location in London. The data center was outfitted with state-of-the-art IT infrastructure specified by our global technology blueprint strategies for server, storage, network, and other infrastructure disciplines. Setting up the data center had taken a tremendous amount of work and planning, including the participation of 300 infrastructure specialists across the globe. Yet, the first business milestone was still ahead: the migration of 1,800 employees from various London-area sites to the new office headquarters location. In addition to moving the employee desktops, systems, and trading floor environments to the location, the team also needed to consolidate and migrate several hundred different business applications located in six local technology centers into one new regional data center. These applications were accessed by thousands of

State Street employees in fourteen different locations and by hundreds of our clients with direct network connections.

Our goal throughout the project was to design and implement a plan that would make the transition entirely invisible to our end-users—customers and employees. They would not know that we did it. We achieved this by analyzing the business processes and understanding the components (people, applications, data and facilities, and more) and interdependencies between them. This provided a detailed foundation for comprehensive migration planning, scheduling and testing, and for contingency plans to ensure rollback capability, if needed. As planned, the team successfully migrated all 1,800 end-users, the several hundred business applications, and hundreds of clients without a single interruption.

Although not all innovation projects face this type of technical and logistical complexity, most do face considerable complexity of some sort. I believe that an innovator's attitude toward such intricacies often determines how successful they will be. Some people get lost in complexity, for example. If they move forward at all, it is painstakingly slow and inefficient. Others dismiss any hint of complexity, irritated with those who may bring it up. They prefer to charge ahead and let the chips fall where they may.

The most successful, I've found, are leaders who move forward with both realism and confidence. They don't try to address all of the complexity on their own. Instead, they structure their team and their plan to do so. They set high standards for performance and ensure that team members develop plans to address the risks and quality issues that might be encountered. They integrate these into a detailed implementation and contingency plan that is communicated to the entire project team and all stakeholders. In other words, effective innovators aim for flawless execution.

Rapid Value Delivery

Quality is just one of the essential elements of effective execution. Timeliness is the other. Timeliness is more than simply being on schedule. It is having a sense of *urgency* about delivering value quickly and effectively. In any endeavor, the sooner we can deliver value, the better. The world is moving much faster. When businesses want something done, they want it done *now*. Technology people must be able to respond with the required speed. This is why rapid value delivery is so important. If we can deliver a portion of the requirements quickly, the business can use that immediately. Then, we can make adjustments along the way instead of waiting until the entire project is completed.

In innovation, when our goal is to establish competitive advantage, speed is even more essential. Clearly, we cannot sacrifice quality to achieve speed. But there are plenty of things we *can* do.

The first is to break a large initiative into smaller phases that each deliver value. This is unlike traditional project planning and execution, where value is delivered at the end after all the individual pieces are brought together. Rapid value delivery, instead, proceeds in a series of small bursts, each of which delivers value to the customer and provides input for the next phase. This is a very important distinction, and one that is not made as often as we might expect. In fact, people with a very clear vision and a comprehensive solution sometimes go about achieving it using a traditional approach. They make very real progress toward their goal, but they do not focus on doing it in a way that creates immediate results and business value. The traditional approach may seem to be a faster, simpler, and surer way to reach their goal, yet it rarely is. There are always complications that we just can't predict, and sometimes we encounter changes that can overturn our original assumptions. Short bursts that quickly bring about immediate benefits will demonstrate the value of our solution and keep us tightly linked with sponsors, customers, and other stakeholders. Each phase, then, becomes more than just another *step* toward our goal. Improvements are experienced at each stage. And our strategy is continually affirmed.

Generally, we want to begin with the quickest win we can find that is able to stand on its own and provide an achievable and valued benefit for our customer. It may be one feature that we can provide to all customers, or it may be new functionality that we can provide for one customer. It doesn't matter if it's small; what matters is whether it provides demonstrable business value, as quickly as possible. This then becomes the scope of that phase.

Leveraging virtualization technology was always a fundamental part of our Blueprint strategy and key to our vision of a 21st Century Technology Infrastructure. We executed against that vision in small but meaningful steps along every front. For example, when a new storage virtualization technology became available, we decided to leverage it for all unstructured data, such as corporate e-mail and personal file storage. This allowed us to consolidate the many local storage environments, which were difficult to manage and recover, and locate them in enterprise or regional data centers.

We began with one data center and a few local buildings in the Boston area to validate the business case and demonstrate the benefits. It was a huge success with plenty of immediate benefits: savings in data center space, utility expenses, technology and facility equipment cost, and staffing cost and improved responsiveness to new business and regulatory requirements globally. Once this phase was completed and the value of the project demonstrated, we continued the project for all buildings, all regions worldwide.

Selecting an appropriate scope is a matter of judgment and experience. However, I find that even very experienced people often start with a scope that is larger than it needs to be. This creates more risk, complexity, and delay than is really necessary.

Too often I've seen what we call *scope creep* take place in projects. Every time a customer or user brings up a suggestion, it's added to the list of items to be completed, without priorities attached. In this way, the project is expanded well beyond the initial requirement. The key in these situations is to prioritize all the requirements in the list based on criticality to the business, and then separate them into phases. Obviously, there should be flexibility in case the business requirements change. Management of the scope requires sound judgment and communications with the customers and project team. Focus is the key. Plus, I always recommend thinking first about the smallest and simplest way to provide value. It may be enough.

After we define scope, we want to take a baseline measurement of current performance or capability. That's not always possible, especially when we're introducing something entirely new. However, as we discussed in Chapter 4, *Promote*, it's important that we do our best to assess our "before" state so that we can have a fact-based "after" comparison. The new solution must be better than the old one if it is to demonstrate value. Whenever possible, we want to quantify in advance the result that our customer wants, expects, and is willing to pay for. That allows us to align our own goals and investment accordingly.

Once we have finalized our scope and determined our baseline, we can use rapid experimentation to test our assumptions and complete a proof-of-concept to validate our approach. Rapid experimentation means giving promising ideas a chance, but doing it in such a way that we minimize up-front investment. In this way, we don't waste limited time, energy, and resources. By quickly putting ideas to the test, we can confirm or dismiss key assumptions up front, and then either accept and integrate the idea or move on to another.

One way we did this at State Street was to establish an Innovation Lab. With the lab in place, we were able to test new technologies in the free thirty- to ninety-day test period offered by many technology companies. We were set up to evaluate the new technologies quickly without buying them, generating metrics and information for our business cases.

The rapid experimentation approach also encourages those who come up with ideas to keep trying, because they know their efforts will be given a chance—even if that chance occurs in a narrow timeframe. The innovator never forgets, however, that while rapid experimentation allows us to fail fast and learn fast with minimal investment, the experiments are performed with meeting project goals in mind. For example, rapid experimentation does not necessarily imply that we're developing throwaway solutions. Our goal is to minimize up-front investment, not waste it! As soon as we know our direction, each step we take is an investment in the future. Having an end-state architecture in mind, even during the early experimental activities, can speed progress and minimize costs as we proceed.

Throughout this process, we must remember that timing is everything. I believe in doing whatever we can to meet our delivery date, with the single exception of cutting corners. There may be ways to prioritize and temporarily omit less critical functionality, and then add it in immediately afterward. When we work with our customer and stakeholders to assess trade-offs like this, we typically arrive at an agreeable solution.

Once we were migrating into a new system which wasn't yet able to meet the processing time allowed to generate certain reports—we were missing the 3:00 A.M. delivery time by 45 minutes. We needed to buy some time before we could tune the system to meet this requirement. We asked the business area exactly when they needed the reports, and they told us by 6:00 A.M. We renegotiated the delivery time to somewhat later than 3:00 A.M., since no one really needed the reports until later anyway.

Similarly, I think it is very important that we never let our focus on speed lead us to dismiss the concerns or ideas of others. There is always time to listen to legitimate concerns and to do what we can to resolve them constructively, in a way that is acceptable to the largest number of stakeholders.

Nor should new ideas, which will come along the way, be dismissed in the name of urgent delivery. New ideas should always be encouraged, and if there is no time to test them at the moment, they can be catalogued and reconsidered later, in the same way that less important functionalities can be added after the primary implementation is complete and the system is operable. In other words, an effective innovator can recognize both issues and opportunities without impacting the delivery timeline.

Managing scope is a critical discipline and a hallmark of those who execute effectively. Good scope management allows us recognize the difference between quality—which we want—and perfectionism—which we usually can't afford. Quality is a matter of achieving zero defects relative to our scope. Perfectionism goes beyond our scope, looking to achieve ends that are not within our current mission. There's nothing inherently wrong with going beyond, unless it threatens to interfere with our goal. Effective innovators ensure that team members focus on achieving the core mission and temporarily shelve additional features that will impact the cost, timeliness, or complexity at that particular stage of the innovation.

Finally, a successfully executed project looks ahead to the needs of those who will use the new solution. The training and education that accompany products and services need to be part of the plan. They are very important to customers, to the sales force, and to all others who have to understand the newly incorporated capabilities so that they will be able to fully utilize them. The developers also need to set up a mechanism for feedback about user friendliness, and it can be built into training programs. That way they can quickly determine how easy or hard it is for people to learn the new product or services.

Putting the Pieces Together

I always like to say, "Quality is not perfectionism, and urgency is not panic." As innovators, we need to develop and exercise the kind of judgment that can help us recognize the difference. We must also recognize that execution is not simply a matter of carrying out the plan. Execution is about *achieving the results*. I think this idea is captured beautifully in the expression "The operation was a success, but the patient died." John Swainson, president of Dell Software, also provides a great industry example:

> Ease and simplicity of use differentiates a successful innovation from one that's unsuccessful. What was fundamentally different between a Zune and an iPod? The technologies were roughly the same. But Zune was hard to use and therefore had relatively low adoption. iPod was easy to use and had higher adoption. So then you got this virtuous circle going on with the iPod because more people were using it, so more of the content providers wanted to make their content available to run on it, which never happened with Zune.

Innovators with advanced skills execute their projects in a way that quickly and closely aligns them to the wants and needs of their customers and markets. They use the twin principles of flawless execution and rapid value delivery to capture the buy-in and enthusiasm of their customers and to continually fine-tune their strategy and approach. Tom Mendoza has an interesting take on the interplay of strategy and execution:

> I have the opportunity to speak at Stanford quite often and one of the mantras of this business teacher there is "Would you

rather have a great strategy or a great execution?" Of course, when your parents have paid that much for college, you say, "Strategy!" But the teacher says that's wrong because if you don't execute you don't even know if you have the right strategy. So I think it is very important at all times to know what is going well and what's not going well. If we find it is not going well, we have to ask ourselves, "What's the real reason? Have we executed perfectly?" If the answer is no, let's make sure we execute perfectly before we change the strategy. But if the answer is yes and it is not working, then we've got to step up and say, "Okay, we are going to change."

Execute: Levels of Effectiveness

Level One: Unproductive

As leaders at Level One, we aim too high or too low. We have difficulty defining or managing the scope of our projects. We tend to oversimplify or overcomplicate. We are rarely in touch with what's actually required by customers and clients. We get "stuck in the mud," unable to maintain focus to bring about desired results.

Level Two: Systematic

When we are operating at Level Two, we use a standard methodology to define and execute structured stages and to manage scope. We have a realistic understanding of what's required and how to get there. We always pilot to test our assumptions. We have developed and use effective project, budget, and issues management processes.

Level Three: Accelerated

At Level Three we are focused on creating demonstrable customer value with each stage. We remember to drive for the quickest wins that can stand on their own. We utilize rapid experimentation and fast failure techniques to test assumptions up front. Finally, we leverage metrics effectively to track, communicate, and celebrate progress.

Server Certification Process

The following is a brief but exemplary story about the power of effective execution. It began with a series of complaints from our application developers about the excessive time needed by the technology infrastructure group to "certify" a server, which included ordering the equipment, installing all the systems and applications products on the system, and connecting the equipment into the test environment for the developers to utilize. In a company the size of State Street, with a vast technology infrastructure, this was no small issue—and what's more, it was a recurring one.

The process in place at that time required developers to begin by submitting a request for an "environment" needed for their application development work. Once that was approved, the infrastructure group began the lengthy process of getting the server hardware and software ready. But after listening to feedback from a number of our internal customers, I assigned a process engineer to review the entire procedure, and to conduct an assessment of its effectiveness and quality control. When we reviewed the engineer's assessment, we saw that there were 108 separate steps in the server certification process. Moreover, it involved several different technology functional areas, with no single owner of the entire process.

So, there were four major issues. The first was the 108 steps, which simply took too long to complete. The second was the waiting time between consecutive steps. The third was that most of the 108 steps were performed manually. Not enough automation was involved. The fourth was that no single functional area *owned* the request and certification process. That meant the request could sit unfulfilled for too long, since no one was accountable, and no one was monitoring the total time it took. So now it was quite obvious that prompt action was necessary. And as innovators, we saw that the "problem" offered us a huge opportunity for improvement.

Immediately, we assembled a global team with representatives from every functional area involved. The team's initial goal was to cut the time needed for the entire process in half and to reduce the number of steps in the process. To reach that goal, we first assigned an owner to the server certification process, creating a new department made up of existing employees, and calling it Server Integration Services. After months of hard work, the team was able to reduce the 108 steps to approximately 52, and to reduce the average elapsed time between a request and a server certification by more than 50 percent. Then, with some further effort, we were able to further reduce the steps down to 25. At that point, I challenged the team to develop a way to have no human intervention at all from the initial requester to final completion and delivery. Our team finally was able to complete any simple server certification request within one hour by total automation with no human intervention. For the more complicated requests, the delivery time became just a few weeks, yielding a tremendous improvement over the old system.

We did continue to use some people for part of the process, but they were assigned to monitor each request and to insure that all requests were processed as quickly as possible. These monitors would notify the functional group in the event that they observed anything slowing down the process. Later on, we were also able to automate much of our monitoring as well, yielding even more savings.

Along the way, we did not stop when we reached our first milestone. Every time the team completed a stage, we immediately established another goal farther down the path. Finally, we set the goal that would have been unimaginable at the beginning of our initiative— the one-hour turnaround from a request to a certified server, without human intervention. And, as I noted earlier, our team eventually achieved it for all simple server certification requests.

Here you can see all the principles at work: listening to identify both a need and an opportunity, leading by tackling the problem, positioning the initiative within the company's cost-cutting strategy, promoting the team's achievements as each milestone was reached, connecting with all the technology teams, committing to a remarkable goal, and finally, executing so flawlessly that the savings and streamlining occurred without any adverse impact on the business.

Execute—Concrete Steps for Putting This Discipline into Action

Individual

Innovators deal effectively with complexity through communication, teamwork, and planning, maintaining a dual focus on flawless execution and rapid value delivery. They work with their stakeholders to assess present positions, design practical solutions, and thoroughly understand the goals, quality requirements, and risks. They proceed in carefully scoped phases, structuring each one around the fastest, most achievable benefit that would be valued by the customer. They leverage experimentation and incorporate the principles of "fail fast" to test and modify their assumptions and strategy. They look for metrics and other fact-based ways to measure and communicate progress, continually improving their approach and solution as they move forward.

Team and Organization

Teams and organizations can formalize processes that incorporate the principles of flawless execution and rapid value delivery. Each of these, of course, first requires that leaders set and communicate the standards for teams and projects. They can then employ practices such as change management reviews, which happen before project execution, and postmortem reviews, which happen afterwards. Change management reviews ensure that project plans account effectively for business and other risks. Postmortem reviews capture the lessons learned during the execution of a project. Teams can even have a "pre-postmortem" review session that involves imagining all of the things that might go wrong and then developing contingency plans accordingly.

How to Execute

✓ Make your vision a reality with determination

✓ Passion creates energy and positive attitude—never give up

✓ Maintain a "laser focus" upon delivery of results and commitment

✓ Assemble the best team with common goals and where everyone is "on a mission"

✓ Pursue "flawless execution"—raise the standards of excellence—always aspire to zero-defect execution

✓ Divide each project into smaller phases, with short-term achievable milestones

✓ Concentrate on key deliverables and circumvent any unexpected issues

✓ Always focus on the key goals—do not get distracted by less important issues

✓ Be flexible for unforeseen events—make sound judgment for alternatives

✓ Establish benchmarks both before and after each project and/or program

✓ Measure, communicate, and celebrate accomplishments immediately

變

Chapter 8

Evolve

We often associate evolution with the theory of biological adaptation and change. That process, as we learned in school, is driven by random mutations, natural selection, and vast amounts of time. Yet when we apply that same term to innovation, the meaning could not be more different. This type of evolution is not something that happens to us, it's something we actively bring about. It can't take long periods of time, or we won't be here to reap the benefits. And it is not about becoming better adapted to our environment. It's about being willing to change the very ground under our feet, again and again.

When I speak to groups about the discipline that I call *Evolve*, people sometimes ask if I think that even innovators have a "natural" resistance to change. As I mentioned in an earlier chapter, though, I actually don't necessarily agree with the concept of *natural* resistance to change. I think there are always reasons for resistance, and the better we understand them, the better able we are to address them. I've mentioned a few of the reasons previously, such as risk of failure, complacency, and the desire to hold on to previous successes.

However, I do believe that innovators themselves can resist change as well. I've seen it happen. Sometimes we were so pleased with the great results we delivered previously that we didn't see a need to change. *And because we didn't see a need, we didn't look for one, either.* I've also seen innovators become so enamored with a certain new idea or solution or approach that they weren't willing to consider one that was even better. Like everyone else, innovators experience times when they are "stuck in the mud." This chapter provides some perspective and recommendations that can help us combat that mind-set in ourselves, our teams, and in our organizations.

Evolve 變 *Bian*

The Chinese concept of the Universe is that things evolve, or change. The only thing that is sure is that change is constantly happening. Evolve or 變 *bian* is central to good governance.

The character for *bian*, falling tone, consists of 言 *yan*, speech flanked on both sides by 絲 *si*, silk threads, pronounced *lian*, above the character which stands for "strike." Change is tangled and difficult and takes effort; sometimes striking quickly is most effective. Or conversely sometimes change "strikes" quickly. So a leader must be prepared to evolve, to change and have multiple plans of action to deal with whatever may strike, or to foster change when the time is ripe.

Footnote: Here the pronunciation indicator works; *lian* rhymes with *bian*.

Overcoming Success

Even when people and organizations fully support and actively pursue change, there are still challenges. It sounds counterintuitive, but success itself often slows momentum. Ming Tsai explains most eloquently how we must handle today's success to avoid inadvertently planting the seeds of tomorrow's failure:

Once you do reach a place—not necessarily at the top, but a place where you are happy—you can't rest on your laurels because, believe me, there's ten other people that would love to be in that spot. And that's where innovation comes in; you have to always be recreating yourself. At Blue Ginger we had a great ten-year run. And then we said okay, let's continue innovating, let's add private dining rooms and a new bar. And when we added a new bar lounge, it gave us that opportunity to add a whole new casual appeal. People could walk in without reservations, wearing blue jeans and shorts and enjoy a Blue Ginger experience, but at half the price. And the private dining allowed us to be more formal. Wedding rehearsals, businesses could hold formal board meetings with dinner, and so forth. So that was a great re-creation and again it put Blue Ginger on the map. People wrote about it, talked about it, and tweeted about it. It was a great way to just remind people about Blue Ginger.

Ten years is a long time. . . . You can be the best in Wellesley and the best in Boston, but you still need to get people to come back. In Boston there are at least five new restaurants every month. And that's nothing like New York, where there are something like 50 new restaurants a month. So you have to know that, and you can't ignore it and just say, "It's okay, I am the best." Well you won't remain the best for very long.

Unfortunately, many formerly great, incredibly innovative companies fall into this trap, not realizing that whatever the thing is in their business creating strategic value *today* may not do so *tomorrow*. Companies like Kodak—the great pioneer in film production—or Blockbuster—the onetime juggernaut video and DVD retailer—come to mind immediately. Kodak, of course, missed the revolution in digital photography, and Blockbuster became vulnerable when the revolution in streamed content occurred. Compare those companies to businesses like Amazon or IBM that keep a steady eye on creating the future, never stop innovating, and continually reinvent themselves.

The same slowing of momentum that success brings can apply in the case of teams and individuals that have achieved some desired change. In both cases, their solutions may succeed in creating business value and competitive advantage, yet too often become the new status quo. Now, as far as these teams or individuals are concerned, making any changes to their great achievements are just as hard as making changes to the solutions that their achievements have replaced. The prevailing attitude can become, "The company just went to all that trouble, didn't it? Now let's buckle down, get to work, and not try to change it over and over again." Others may say, "See, we support innovation around here, and now that it's done, let's get back to our real business. After all, we've solved the problem. We're doing things differently—better. It's more efficient, costs less, and gives us all sorts of functionality we never had before. Why change now?"

Tom Mendoza, vice chairman of NetApp, points out that the role of leaders in making sure complacency never sets in can be furthered by good questioning skills—questions that encourage others to put their best thinking forward and not fall into the trap of thinking that enough is good enough.

> A good leader probes to make people really think about their solutions. The art of questioning is that you're not threatening anybody, you are not dictatorial, but you are making sure that they understand you want a well-thought-out solution, not just something that is comfortable—because comfort leads to no innovation. Comfort leads to complacency. You may have a piece of your business that is very solid and you just want to just reap it, but you have to keep inventing and innovating if you are going to grow. You have to embrace change. You are either getting better or you are getting worse. If you stay the same, you are getting worse.

Leaders play a critically important role in creating and sustaining the engine of *continual innovation*, especially when team members are enjoying their hard-earned success. Discerning judgment and the sensitivity of emotional intelligence is needed to fuel continued progress in a way that also honors achievement. Again, Tom Mendoza has insights to share:

When things are going well, you need to inject tension, you need to challenge. Complacency is the number one killer of companies. Feeling that everything is okay and we don't have to keep pushing—that's where it all starts to go wrong. And when times are challenging, you need to provide support. As long as you have the right team and they are doing all the right things, you have got to make sure that they understand you are supporting them. I think most companies do exactly the opposite. When times are good, they are slapping everyone on the back, and when times get tough, they inject tension, which helps nobody.

Success is not achieved by arriving at the right solution to a single problem, or reaching your immediate objectives. Enduring success is achieved by sustaining an innovative culture and process which will continually evolve leading-edge solutions and superior results.

There is one more important situation that innovators who evolve have managed to master. It is our ability to learn from others who have succeeded where we have not. Most of us can learn rather quickly from other people's mistakes. However, it is much more difficult for us to learn from other's *successes*. Is it caused by jealousy, perhaps? I'm not certain, but when this situation occurs, it often triggers a natural defensiveness that can lead us to overlook the value or validity of what they have produced. This type of response is not unusual, yet it's completely unnecessary and counterproductive. I've always believed that it's best to avoid defensiveness of any kind, since it rarely helps and usually hurts. For innovators, however, defensiveness simply keeps us from incorporating new insights and improvements into our own results.

Dr. Tenley Albright provides a great example in which reexamining an existing solution yielded new insights and significantly improved results. It was the first major project undertaken by MIT Collaborative Initiatives, done in partnership with the Harvard Graduate School of Design. The project focused on assessing stroke care. As Tenley explains:

We decided not to have a physician or a neurologist or a surgeon lead the project. We decided instead to have an architect and designer from the Harvard School of Design, because architects and designers know how to look at the whole system. In medicine we're always drilling down deeper and deeper and deeper to study things. But here was a situation where the important thing was to step back and look at it broadly, analyzing it from a systems point of view. Designers and architects, like our lead Professor Marco Steinberg, know how to do that. As he put it, we needed to unpack the problem so we could know what we didn't know. So it was a new way of looking at a problem that most people thought had already been solved. Yet we came out of the process with a number of new realizations and ways to improve care. By revising the triage process, for example, we could better respond to the patient's individual needs. This change is now saving lives and decreasing costs.

Going Further Beyond

As innovation leaders, our job is to continue to inspire everyone to search for opportunities to innovate, and reward those who never stop looking for opportunities to improve every aspect of the business. By measuring and communicating results, and by earning industry-wide recognition, we can inspire a continuing cycle of innovation that is driven by its own momentum.

The Rapid Value Delivery methodology described in Chapter 7, *Execute*, also provides a natural vehicle for sustaining the momentum of continual innovation. The goal is to have everyone so excited about the possibilities that open up as each phase is completed that they quickly go about identifying new ideas and improvements that can ride on the most recent change's back. I can recall many projects where exactly that happened. Even before we were done with the core innovation, our engineers were identifying new features and capabilities that would deliver additional business value. With the right support, and the right incentives, those around us will collaborate and compete to discover the next opportunity to improve and change.

Tarkan Maner, previous CEO of Wyse Technology, serial entrepreneur, and investor, puts the concept in a historical context:

> One of my favorite mottos is *plus ultra*. It means "further beyond" in Latin. There is a myth from ancient times that Hercules had erected two columns at the Straits of Gibraltar to mark the edge of the world, which was thought to be flat. And so Mediterranean sailors were warned *non plus ultra*— nothing further beyond these columns, and they didn't sail past them thinking they'd fall off the face of the earth and die. So *non plus ultra* was a warning, but it also meant the ultimate place, the last possible achievement.
>
> After Columbus sailed past those columns, sailed west to reach the east, and instead discovered a new world, Carlos V of Spain adopted the columns for the flag. But he changed the motto to *plus ultra*, meaning always go further beyond. Don't stop achieving and discovering. I always say to myself that life is a marathon, but you're never racing against someone else. You're racing against yourself to find the next opportunity and do something that others did not have the courage or the vision to do.

I learned an important lesson about going further beyond when I was just a girl. When my three sisters and I received permission from the Shanghai local government to visit our parents and our brother for a summer vacation in Hong Kong and go cruising on my father's ship to other Asian countries, we packed one single suitcase for all of us and left everything else behind. We certainly assumed we would be coming home again. However—perhaps subconsciously—I must have been concerned that we might not return, because the only other thing I brought with me was my stamp collection, which I adored. For years, I devoted myself to collecting beautiful multicolored Olympic stamps with all kinds of sports figures. My stamp collection was filled with colorful pictures from exotic lands, such as Olympic skaters in vivid costumes. Since my sister, Margo and I were very athletic, we played basketball, volleyball, and softball, and I also did gymnastics. So the possession I cherished most was my Olympic stamp collection.

At the border station, I watched proudly as the uniformed agent took a special interest in my album, almost expecting to see him demonstrate his admiration with an appreciative nod. Instead, he confiscated my collection.

At first, I stood there frozen in shock, trying to comprehend what he had just done. As my understanding dawned, I began crying, pleading between sobs for him to return my stamps. He was unrelenting, however, and sternly announced that valuables could not leave the country. I begged him to let me send the collection to my grandmother in Shanghai, but he just shook his head, shouted, "No!" and motioned me on. I continued wailing as my sisters hurried me away and across the border. Even today, I can easily retrieve the grief and helplessness of that moment when I lost something in which I had invested so much time, effort, and passion. Thankfully, this happened as I literally crossed into "a new land of hope and opportunity." Once I reached Hong Kong, I was amazed to find that, everywhere I looked, I saw the same colorful vibrancy that I had loved so much in my stamps! This pivotal and formative experience taught me that change—going "further beyond"—sometimes demands the surrender of our greatest treasures, yet we often gain more than we can even imagine.

Over the course of my career, I have seen countless people go to extraordinary lengths to hang on to whatever "stamp book" they hold dear. What I mean is that, too often they seem to prefer the satisfaction brought by existing accomplishments over the challenge and promise of the future. They're not doing this intentionally, of course. They're just happy with whatever they possess here and now, and they are unaware of what's on the other side.

As innovation leaders, we can help people let go of the "stamp books" by sharing in their thrill of victory with each accomplishment—and then encouraging them onto the next. Sometimes, we must do the same for ourselves as well! Each of us can benefit by maintaining a strong conviction that "the best is yet to come!"

Continual Innovation, Not Constant Change

If there's anything better than Ming's butterfish, which I love and have eaten many times at his Blue Ginger restaurant, it's the fact that his insights into his own business apply so widely to others as well. When I spoke with Ming about the concept of *Evolve*, he described how it applies to fine dining. Across the industry, he explained, chefs usually change their menus when the seasons change. This allows them to incorporate different fruits, vegetables, and other items that are in season. In addition:

> Sometimes you innovate because you don't want a menu with just steak and potatoes on it. Other times you want to impress your chef friends, you want something that people in your industry will enjoy. But mostly you innovate because you have to keep it fresh. At least 50 percent of my customers are here a minimum of once a month, and they'll tire of the menu if we don't keep innovating. Still, I always say, don't change something because it feels good to change. Change something because it's a better dish.

For Ming, there is business value in introducing variety. This isn't often the case for businesses, of course. More typically, customers consider change to be a disruption. However, even in a dining establishment where change and variety is inherently desirable, Ming still upholds a standard of continuous improvement. Not just good, better. *We don't change just for the sake of change*, Ming explained. *We change to be better.*

This critically important point is fundamental to the discipline of *Evolve*. It's not about continual change; it's about continual innovation. And, as we have said throughout the book, we define that as creating business value and increasing competitive advantage.

Gerald Chertavian, founder of Year Up, has implemented a formal process for building continual innovation into his organization:

> Internally, we try to institutionalize innovation every six months. We have something we call intersession after every class graduates, for about a month, where we get together as a group city by city. We talk about what went right, what went wrong, what should we change for the next class. There are no sacred cows. Typically we try to talk strictly about the issues—what's been done right and what's been done wrong without casting blame on individuals for making mistakes or

for bad judgment. We just stay focused on what's best for students.

In addition, every six months we take a hard look at the program as a whole to see what innovations might be relevant. So we balance capturing and standardizing on best practice while continuing to allow innovation where we know we still have a lot to learn.

In this discussion, Gerald brings up the important concept of standardization and its use as a vehicle for improvement. By identifying and implementing best practices, organizations improve quality and consistency while reducing cost and complexity. They also create a baseline for future improvement. Yet, as Gerald discusses further below, standardizing too rigidly can accomplish the opposite effect:

For any multisite organization it's a constant tension between where you allow or even incent differentiation and where you require standardization. It's a constant evaluation process. I think you can develop some frameworks for how to think about it, but they're constantly changing in response to the organization's needs. We feel that the absolutely most important things to standardize on are culture, values, and operating principles. Our six values are stated and appointed in every place in the organization you can look, and most decisions are tied back to those values. We have three operating principles: high support, high expectations, and high service. We ask every single leader to demonstrate those operating principles on a daily basis and hold others accountable for doing the same. We also believe in standardizing data. If you have a certain amount of standardization on data, you can drive process control. If you can drive process control, you can drive quality. So it's a lot easier to say "enter data this way," and it's apparent when someone hasn't. You get quality control without having to impose it by actually focusing on data. Centralization of data helps define a better organization. I want people to be able to focus on educational outcomes and let the local site adapt to its market. If you consistently focus on values, operating principles, and data, then you don't have to control what people do on a micro level, which would just stifle their creativity and take away their autonomy and motivation.

Gerald's approach to standardization provides a firm foundation while encouraging continual innovation and customization to local requirements. As he discusses further below, his approach also leverages distributed experimentation in a way that helps the company determine enterprise-level standards:

> We're thinking right now about learning management systems and how we can integrate technology into the curriculum. We're asking ourselves about whether we give each instructor some incentive or capital to try various types of educational technology or just identify a central system to push into the organization.
>
> Given how nascent we are in the educational technology industry, my instinct is to let early adopters come in and support them, hold them up, recognize them. And then over time, figure out what we should standardize around for educational technology. I think the maturity of the industry is obviously going to play a role in determining whether you want innovation happening and how deeply you want that to go.

Clearing the Path

In prior chapters, we discussed the importance of making innovation a part of everyone's routine and every employee's obligation to his/her business, and not relegating it solely to research and development or to business strategists. But with day-to-day operations—putting out the fires and just keeping the operation running smoothly—as the focus of most of our time, attention, and energies, how do we do this?

Jim Phalen of State Street describes the challenge and how he is addressing it by opening up the company's strategic planning processes, inviting ideas and contributions from its global employee base.

I have incredible respect for middle managers. They run the show. When you need to make a change, when you get down to the hard work, they are the people that do it. Many organizations leave innovation to their managers. Sure, they can contribute tremendously, but usually, they are the ones trying to keep the trains running on time. We put incredible pressure on them, and the message they get from us, in most organizations, is usually about not messing up.

You can take these managers out of their day-to-day twice a month and ask them to innovate, but unless you are in a crisis, you are probably not going to get big new ideas, and you shouldn't expect to. That's not their failure. We've focused them on protecting the downside rather than building the upside. We haven't pushed the chair back far enough for them to say, tell me what you can do if you are fully automated. Don't think about your process being 10 percent better, think about it being 400 percent better, or totally different, where maybe you don't even do that process anymore.

I think one of the most important things is figuring out how you are going to get those out-of-the-box ideas and combine them with the great manager who can help refine and build on them. So, at State Street, we're engaging all of our employees worldwide in the process of innovation, rather than just the middle managers. In a way, it's putting more pressure on our middle managers because we've gone below them as well as above them. But we are trying to open up the process. It's not about finding problems; it's about finding ways to be even better than we are today.

Through the use of collaboration tools, social media, and innovation rally events, State Street employees are forming and joining communities that cross functional, geographic, and business boundaries. Communities focus on business topics such as products, services, markets, and customers as well as internal topics such as sustainability and flexible work. Nearly 70 percent of State Street employees have some type of flexibility in their schedule, so it is a particularly active community. Members support each other by answering questions and suggesting strategies, and the "wisdom of the crowd" elevates the best program improvement ideas for consideration by the corporate support team. Like Year Up, State Street is leveraging this distributed yet still collective intelligence to identify and implement continual innovation.

IBM, through many years, has created one of the best-known innovation machines, establishing the kind of culture where change is the norm rather than the exception, and innovation has become business-as-usual. Linda Sanford, IBM's senior vice president, Enterprise Transformation, explains IBM's systemic approach to moving forward and never resting on its laurels:

> Creating a culture that values innovation is part of IBM's DNA—from the earliest days when company founder Thomas Watson embraced the term "Think" to inspire creativity from his teams, to the present when innovation has become a cultural underpinning and competitive advantage. Innovation is a by-product of hard work, creativity, skill, and delivering support to develop ideas. Advancing this environment is paramount at IBM.
>
> With an R&D investment that has held steady at around $6 billion a year, IBM is one of the world's biggest proponents of "ground-up" innovation—a philosophy that has produced everything from the relational database to Watson, the computer system capable of fielding natural language questions. Giving creative minds the space to explore big ideas is the norm at IBM.
>
> So is celebrating innovation. Each year, the company names new IBM Fellows and Distinguished Engineers to honor those who have made significant contributions while giving them additional resources to continue innovating. We give a lot of visibility to our outstanding innovators and our next generation technologists aspire to reach the same heights.
>
> In addition, the company's Technology Adoption Program is a community of employees who exchange new applications and technical ideas and consider their value to the marketplace. Ideas that show the most promise are funded for development.

Since we started this program in 2005, more than 1,500 applications have been piloted through this program. It's been a great way for our technologists to get real-time feedback on their applications.

Regularly, IBM also holds "HackDay"—an open forum for employees to share for solving business and IT challenges. A recent HackDay explored how IBM could expand as a social business, looking at broader ways to use Facebook, Twitter, and even IBM's own social media community, Connections.

Adversity and Change

Of course, success is not the only cause of innovators digging in their heels. As the inventor and entrepreneur Nathan Myhrvold described in Chapter 6, *Commit*, one of the greatest challenges an innovator faces is being able to recognize the difference between when it's time to keep pushing forward and when it's time to stop. There's no formula, Nathan indicated, other than asking yourself what you would do at that moment if you were just starting from scratch. If you hadn't already invested so much in that effort, would you do it now?

As discussed in earlier chapters, a culture that avoids penalizing failure provides a necessary foundation for asking and answering a question like that. Tom Mendoza, who established that type of culture at NetApp, acknowledges that the question is difficult, yet the answer is sometimes very clear:

> Sometimes you just have to change because if you keep going in the same direction you are going to lose. You have got to be honest about it. I think the worst thing you can do is to have a culture where you can't say that we are losing. You need a culture of safety, where as long as you are doing what you think is right for the company, not for personal gain or advancement, then you put it on the table. You need to be honest about what really is working and what's really not working. And if something is not working, the company has to accept that.

During the banking slowdown, for example, we had a lot of endeavors underway. We had an offsite and took a look at these projects to see if they were the right investments given what we knew was going to happen to the economy and the banking sector. I don't believe in the approach where, when things get bad, everybody cuts their budgets by 20 percent. You might end up cutting the area that could innovate you out of the problem by 20 percent, and you're cutting something that is going to be worthless by 20 percent too.

So, instead, we said, if we had a lot more money, where would be put it *now*. There was amazing consensus about where we'd all make a big bet. Then we said, okay, we don't have a lot more money, so what three things are we going to *stop* investing in so we can get it? Again—we got amazing consensus. We stopped all three that were identified, and one meant having to sell off a company we had bought less than a year before. That was painful, and it certainly affected people in that room. We just said, "You know what, given the new reality, that investment's not going to pay off. We are not going to spend the next five years grooming it, we are going to sell it, and we are going to take that investment and put it somewhere else."

Like Nathan, Tom and his executive team found that they needed to consciously and deliberately set aside the financial and emotional investments of the past. In a culture that does not penalize failure, this can be done. Shedding and learning from the mistakes of the past makes a great deal of sense. In a culture where past mistakes significantly impact future prospects, however, it is a much more difficult task to accomplish.

Regardless of the culture that we find ourselves in, it's hard to admit that we don't have all of the answers. It takes strong leadership to admit mistakes and take action to fix them. This is much harder to do than to just keep going until it is too late. Quick action on this front will keep the business from wasting more investment money and not getting the expected returns.

As much as I dislike the concept of *natural* resistance to change, I do believe that human beings have a natural resistance to changing *ourselves* and our *beliefs*. It can be done, but it is hard work, as Dr. Eugene Chan can attest. In Chapter 2, Dr. Chan, founder of the DNA Medicine Institute and several other startup companies, told us that he had never truly appreciated the positive lessons that can be learned from failure until half of his company quit. He completely changed his understanding of what leadership means and changed himself as a result.

It was a *personal* evolution, which is very hard for most people. I have to say that if that early leadership failure of mine hadn't happened, there's a chance that even to this day I wouldn't realize what I was doing wrong. But it was one of those times where you just have to be reflective and you have to evolve. You have to think, "Hey, am I doing something wrong here?" So I thought about it, and I knew that it wasn't as though these employees were all bad and so that's why they left the company. *Something must be wrong with me.*

It's very difficult to see the things that you don't know about yourself. But by shouldering that blame and doing the introspection, you learn. And I have to say that it's been amazing and it's been transformative. It made me so much more effective at doing what I do.

I think any failure is filled with huge learning opportunities if you're willing to examine it rather than just brush it off. There's no better way to be better.

And if you don't take advantage of those opportunities, the issue is just going to come up again. And I think this is true for organizations as a whole as well as for people.

I couldn't agree more. In fact, the same viewpoint was described in Chapter 6, *Commit*, by Admiral Mullen, who almost ended his career when he crashed his first ship. I believe that, as innovators and as people, our response to adversity is the single most important determiner of our success. The question isn't whether or not we will experience it, because adversity is inevitable. The question is what we will do when it happens. Will we view the challenges it poses as a motivator, a way to help us learn and evolve, or will we see it as an enemy and hunker down instead?

Challenges and adversity are everywhere and if we do not learn to deal with them, we will be at a disadvantage in all aspects of our lives and careers. I once heard a successful executive talk about her belief that the term *career path* sets improper expectations for young people entering the work force. She believed that it gave young people the impression that a pathway was already carved out and that all that was required on their part was to follow it. "They should call it a 'career obstacle course' instead." she joked, so that people would go into their careers knowing that their progress would depend on their ability to move past the problems and difficulties that life will put in their way.

I thought about her comment when I chose the name for this book, *The Innovator's Path*. I've mentioned it earlier in the book, and by now I'm quite sure that readers know full well that their path to innovation is not already cut out for them. They are the ones doing the cutting; they are the ones leading the way. Leading innovation requires passion, a positive attitude and outlook, and a strong conviction to avoid wasting time on the negative. When we encounter challenges, we first try to turn them around, transforming problems into opportunities and adversaries into allies. When that's not possible, we don't waste our time in battle; we work around that which we cannot control or change. Doing so requires skillful leadership and connection, but it's worth the time and will be a huge win for the team, for the organization, and for ourselves.

I have had the great pleasure of attending several of Dean Kamen's FIRST events. Dean is helping to create and energize our next generation of innovators. I believe that his approach to putting kids in situations where they have to "cut their own paths" has important lessons for us all.

FIRST is about showing kids that innovation, even though you fail a lot, is fun, it is exciting, and it is worth the failures. And at FIRST we work really, really, really hard to give kids problems to which they can't go find the answer in the back of a book. We give them a pile of junk and a problem statement. And we work all year on creating the problem statements and the pile of junk. . . . We continue to add complexity to all the problem statements until a whole bunch of "smart people" would all violently disagree on what is the "right answer," because the whole point is, there is no right answer to most problems. There's no best solution to real problems, because there's an infinite number of different ways that you can add imagination to all the tools in your box and come up with something that's never been done before. And that's exciting.

Now, as I've done throughout this book, I'll ask each reader to evaluate him or herself on the scale of effectiveness below.

Evolve: Levels of Effectiveness

Level One: Satisfied

At Level One we are fully content with recent efforts and achievements and are enjoying a sense of completion and pride. We are feeling comfortable and secure with the company's current strategic and competitive position and the role we've played in both.

Level Two: Pacing

At Level Two we are pleased with recent efforts and achievements but are open to ongoing change and improvement. We are continually monitoring the company's strategic and competitive position and remain alert for the need to make changes.

Level Three: Driving

At Level Three we've already moved on! We are actively seeking and implementing change and improvement. We are making a major impact on the company recognizing that innovation should be a part of every business process. We are continually seeking ways to enhance strategic value and improve our competitive position.

Evolving from Certification to Cloud

In Chapter 7, *Execute*, I discussed our server certification process as an example of a project with rapid value delivery. We responded to customer needs, taking a difficult problem and making the solution incrementally better and better. This chapter, *Evolve*, allows me to pick up where I left off and demonstrate the principle of leaving our good work behind.

In some ways, our Server Integration Services team had a thankless role, as functions that come into play at the tail end of a process are often at a disadvantage. They're not always included in planning and design discussions and must therefore play "catch up" before they can contribute meaningfully. They often find that key decisions have already been made and cast in stone, despite the fact that they could have offered even better solutions. Yet, because they know that by that point in time their input would just be perceived as a complaint, they do their best to grin and bear it. And, to make matters worse, most of the contingency time in the project schedule has already been used up, so they are also typically racing against the clock.

As I described in Execute, the team did a great job coming up with an automated one-hour server certification solution that dramatically accelerated their response time. However, it could only be used for standard requests. When servers required customization, which they very often did, the process could still take weeks. As Nathan Myhrvold told us in Chapter 1, *Listen*, Henry Ford did not try to make a faster horse. He recognized that any *significant* improvement from that point on would require an entirely new solution. We recognized that as well.

We began implementing a solution in our data center that we called POD, for Processing on Demand, which is a standardized and pre-built environment. This was a container-like design that unified network, server, storage, and even air conditioning. Each POD was its own virtualized environment built around a core of seven cabinets, for 63 servers in a POD. A POD could be quickly deployed without the usual connectivity challenges of individual components. And because of the multiserver and storage virtualization, more capacity was easily available to applications, requiring fewer new servers to be certified. Although the terms *cloud computing environment* and *infrastructure-as-a-service* were not widely used then, these were the very same concepts underlying our POD solution.

Of course, the full value of this solution could only be realized in a fully standardized environment. We worked closely with State Street's IT Architecture group to achieve that vision. Using POD as the foundation, the team developed a standardized application services platform that allowed developers to use self-service rather than certification to provision their application environments. An automated workflow manages the authorization approvals and, in minutes, the system automatically provisions the desired application environment, doing so in a highly resilient active/active configuration across two data centers. In addition to infrastructure-as-a-service, we now have platform-as-a-service, software-as-a-service, business services and information services, with each layer standardized and prebuilt.

This private cloud architecture is retooling and reframing the way that State Street's entire IT function operates, introducing an unprecedented degree of speed, resiliency, cost-effectiveness, and control. In addition to providing a significant return on IT investment, it is heightening State Street's capacity for rapid innovation and providing a launching point for several strategic new business services, such as a self-service data warehouse and extended analytic data services.

Evolve—Concrete Steps for Putting This Discipline into Action

Let's turn now to our summary of *Evolve* in the context of the individual and the team and organization.

Individual

Continual innovation for the individual means producing results and celebrating success, yet never allowing ourselves to be content with what we have achieved. We can maintain a mind-set of "the best is yet to come" and constantly search out ways to be better. This applies to how we respond to adversity as well. We always stay positive and do not waste time on things we cannot control. Innovators don't defend themselves against opportunities to learn; they seek them out.

Team and Organization

Teams often bond around the great accomplishments that they produce, yet this bonding can produce a new and rigid status quo. The role of the team leader, therefore, is critical. We have to be open to suggestions for doing things differently, reward questions as much as answers, and encourage new ideas. In so doing, we continually encourage the team to move forward and out of its comfort zone.

An organization's culture should be one that inspires and encourages people to continually innovate. This requires executive focus and structured processes that continually examine existing solutions and challenge people to think about ways to improve them. The organization should implement practices that instill and/or reinforce the idea of "innovation-as-usual."

How to Evolve

✓ "The important race is always with yourself" (Tarkan Maner)

✓ Inspire and create a culture of continuous improvement—maintain your momentum

✓ Never become complacently satisfied with your prior successes

✓ Rotate people through different assignments to continually challenge them with fresh perspectives

✓ Always look for the next new ideas and opportunities for continuous improvement

✓ Uncover and evaluate strategic future plans, from all available sources—suppliers, vendors, partners, venture capitalists, startups, and the like

✓ To remain competitive, you need to be continuously evolve

✓ Reward people for continuous innovation and creating business value

✓ Measure and communicate loudly and broadly for results from designed destruction

✓ "The Best Is Yet to Come"

Afterword

I believe that change (改变—*gai bian*) is our bridge to the future, and we should always cross it confidently, without looking back. Yet this writing journey has allowed me to do both—to try something new and to look back, both at the same time.

Looking back across the many decades of my career rekindled so many episodes of challenge and delight. Three marvelous companies offered me opportunities that a Chinese-born girl of my generation would never have dared to dream of. Many great leaders taught me everything I've written in this book and gave me the greatest gifts I have ever received—a passion to make a difference and a will to win.

Looking back at my time at State Street, I see how dozens of standalone infrastructure groups joined together to be united into one single, forward-looking global organization. I see worldwide teams that are now guided by a shared technology blueprint, unified by common processes, and driven by clear business priorities. I see sound skills and practices that have become second nature: an expert focus on business value and measurement, optimization, zero-defect execution, and rapid innovation. I see all of the challenges we overcame, the goals we achieved, the accolades we earned, and the fun we shared. We are so proud and honored that State Street is "Best in Class" and optimally positioned for cloud computing, big data, and analytics.

Looking back at my time in the chief innovation officer's role, I see our small yet elite team of experienced staff members, students, and young rising stars. We championed, created, and evolved tools and practices such as State Street's innovation collaboration community, bringing innovation into prominent focus for every employee, advancing a tradition of innovation to become an integral part of State Street's "business-as-usual."

I hope all eight disciplines prove as valuable for many other individuals, teams, and organizations as they have for me and my team. As we all embark on our future evolutionary transformations, I urge every one of us to always remember to find joy and humor in confronting the challenges on each day of our journey!

★   ★   ★

Now, I would like to share my favorite—most memorable—quotation, which is often used to inspire future military officers facing formidable objectives. But it is just as relevant to our work as innovators:

Risk more than others think is safe.
Care more than others think is wise.
Dream more than others think is practical.
Expect more than others think is possible.

Appendix I

The Eight Disciplines—Summaries and Action Plans

聽 Listen

Listening—what could be easier or more routine? Well, I'm sorry to say that neither is true! Listening is difficult and done surprisingly rarely. But the riches we can uncover—and the difficulties we can avoid—when we learn to really listen are incalculable.

Listening is a natural ability in people. We were all born with it. However, the listening I am talking about is an art and a technique: listen to learn, listen deeply, listen effectively, listen wholeheartedly, listen with an open mind and without judgment or presumption. Listen not only to every word the person is saying, but also listen to what is not said. Listen, assemble, and analyze!

Based on my many years of management experience, there are three different levels of effectiveness for listening. The more effectively we listen, the more we learn, and the more productive we can be as we set out to accomplish new goals.

Listen: Levels of Effectiveness

Level One: Selective Listening. At Level One we listen only to information that meets our immediate agenda. Often, under the guise of listening, this level can take the form of frequent interruptions and narrowly focused questions designed only to elicit answers consistent with our interests, not to enlarge our knowledge. At this level, we listen only for what we want to hear, and interpret what is said from our viewpoint alone.

Level Two: Engaged Listening. We reach Level Two when we engage in productive back-and-forth discussions, listening to the viewpoints of others and often expanding our own understanding as a result. At this level, respectful give-and-take dialogue results in acquiring knowledge and producing creative outcomes and helps build long-term relationships.

Level Three: Deep Listening. At Level Three we go beyond *what* is being said to *why* it is being said. We probe deeper, uncover individual assumptions, and seek fresh approaches and new information. We also read body language and may notice patterns that not even the speaker is aware of, which help us gain more insight into his or her true message and motivations. At this level, we are also listening to what is *not* being said.

Listen—Concrete Steps for Putting This Discipline into Action

Individual. First and foremost, we ourselves must change our own behavior and become listeners rather than hearers. Listening, unlike hearing, is not a natural act, and we must learn to listen and choose to listen. I'm always surprised by the reaction I get from people when I talk about this. They get it. They usually grasp the idea immediately and seem genuinely interested in honing their listening skills—especially when they see that by listening, they will discover opportunities and benefit from the insights of others. One of the best ways to develop better listening skills is to pay special attention to our reaction to disconfirming data—information that is at odds with what we think or believe. The usual response is to ignore or dismiss it. Sometimes we argue against it. When we're listening, we actively pursue it with curiosity, humility, and respect.

Team and Organization. To get a team listening, team leaders can suggest practices like "listening to the voice of the customer," designed to gather input regularly, and then to act on it. They can also be encouraged to implement regular information-sharing processes that keep them in touch with changes happening inside and outside of the organization. Most importantly of all, in every team, there are those who do most of the talking and those who do very little. Team leaders can make a special effort to ensure that every member of the team weighs in with their thoughts on important topics and to monitor the ensuing discussion closely to help encourage thoughtful and respectful listening.

At the organizational level, executive leaders must themselves demonstrate this type of advanced listening. They should take care to appoint people with open minds and good listening skills charged with creating an environment that encourages people to communicate honestly and openly. They can work to identify and break down barriers to listening—between individuals, teams, divisions, management, customers, and partners.

How to Listen
- ✓ Show respect for the speaker—maintain eye contact
- ✓ Clear and open your mind and heart to listen—give the speaker your full attention
- ✓ Do not have preconceived expectations regarding what you are about to hear
- ✓ Don't judge as the speaker speaks, but question when you don't understand
- ✓ Never assume what the speaker will say—ask questions to clarify before making assumptions
- ✓ Make sure you understand exactly what every word means

(continued)

✓ Never interpret until the entire message is heard
✓ Look for new information in the conversation
✓ Make the discussion about the speaker's beliefs, not yours
✓ Control your body language—do not cross arms, or signal boredom or a closed mind
✓ Preserve your facial expression—with a little smile for encouragement; do not express disappointment or impatience on your face
✓ Notice the speaker's body language. Look for clues as to *why* he or she is telling you this, not just what
✓ Reflect on what you were told. Look for the root cause and validate with other data
✓ Look at any data you have to see how it compares to what you've been told

領 Lead

There is no single skill more essential to an innovator than knowing how to lead. And the best innovator is always a leader—there is no better way to innovate. However, the full set of leadership skills comes more naturally to some than to others.

When I think about a good leader, I think about someone who is a role model . . . someone we can look up to . . . someone we would like to be when we "grow up" . . . someone we all respect.

These are the characteristics of leaders, especially a leader who is also an innovator:

Passion—passion to lead and a will to win
Vision—a sense of tomorrow
Integrity—most important for sustained leadership
Trust—people will not follow someone who they cannot trust
Urgency—dedication to speed-to-market is critical for an innovator
Results oriented—only the results are valuable, not the efforts expended
Adaptability—ability to continuously anticipate and lead change

Empathy/emotional intelligence—soft skills essential for building connections and relationships

Communication—it is vital to have good verbal and written skills

Confidence—self-confidence is necessary to gain people's trust

Pursuit of excellence—a leader has to set high standards for people to reach

Lead: Levels of Effectiveness

Level One: Limits Ingenuity. At Level One we are limiting ingenuity, often acting as the "brain" and treating others as arms and legs that are there strictly to execute instructions. We are incapable of inspiring others with a clear vision or allowing others to feel a sense of ownership. Leaders at this level are unable to gain the trust and respect of others. Solutions are implemented in a way that generates a "compliance mentality" and fails to bring about desired change. We are unaware of the ways in which the business's existing incentives encourage people to remain tied to the status quo.

Level Two: Leverages Ingenuity. At Level Two we are doing much better, leveraging ingenuity, communicating a clear and achievable short-term vision, and creating enthusiasm, ownership, and accountability. We are able to gain the trust and respect of others through demonstrated integrity. We involve others in designing and implementing solutions, increasing buy-in and reducing resistance. There is a focus on enhancing or supplementing incentives (e.g., compensation) to support accountability, initiative, and teamwork and to minimize penalties for limited risk-taking and failure.

Level Three: Cultivates Ingenuity. At Level Three we are at the top of our game, cultivating ingenuity, upholding a compelling future vision and a strong sense of shared purpose. We always inspire others to do and be their best. We align incentives, social cues, and processes to encourage and manage creativity and change. Emotionally intelligent and highly regarded, this leader challenges and supports others in achieving beyond their own expectations, and actively supports processes that enable experimentation, constructive failure, and learning.

In many organizations, the passion and ingenuity of employees go untapped. Leaders at every level have the opportunity to harness incredibly abundant yet often underutilized resources. Such efforts will not be wasted. As Admiral Mullen told me, "People get a tremendous amount of personal satisfaction with a job well done, with the opportunity to create, to give back, to make a difference. You need to cultivate that. If innovative people do not have a leader to connect to, they are going to go somewhere else."

Lead—Concrete Steps for Putting This Discipline into Action

Individual. Leaders exist at every level of the organization, not just in the management and executive ranks. John Quincy Adams, the sixth president of the United States, said it best: "If your actions inspire others to dream more, learn more, do more, and become more, you are a leader." Leaders articulate a clear vision and invite others to share their passion. They set high expectations and support others in achieving them. Leaders build trust, respect, and integrity by demonstrating it. They work hard to develop emotional intelligence and sound judgment, learning from every experience and emulating the leaders they most admire.

Team and Organization. Innovative cultures encourage experimentation and learning. They do that by ensuring that their expectations, processes, and incentives are all closely aligned. Clear guidelines for acceptable risks are communicated to employees, and people who do the right thing the right way are not punished when they don't get the "right" results. In fact, they're rewarded for their willingness to advance progress. Processes exist to ensure that the organization as a whole is able to learn and benefit from their experience.

How to Lead
- ✓ Possess a passion to lead and a will to win!
- ✓ Show integrity, energy, urgency, positivity, self-confidence, trustworthiness, and compassion
- ✓ Define an innovative vision—a sense of tomorrow

- ✓ Create a culture for innovation—lead by example, encourage, inspire, and reward innovation
- ✓ Initiate changes; take calculated risks fearlessly
- ✓ Communicate effectively with all stakeholders inside and outside the organization—knowing what to say to whom, how, and when
- ✓ Exercise sound judgment and emotional intelligence—understand the proper timing for saying and doing everything
- ✓ Bring a positive attitude to solving challenges. There's always a way; if not, we build the way
- ✓ Earn respect; don't rely on compulsion or an official title
- ✓ Strive to make a difference—focus on your legacy and create enduring strategic value

計 Position

Position means proactively getting ready for future needs. It is how we move from where we are to where we want to be, defining an agile and competitive business model and a strategic roadmap for achieving our future vision and goals. Positioning is vitally important for sustaining competitiveness and remaining successful.

Positioning applies to individuals personally and to the enterprise itself.

For personal positioning, innovators must have a specific goal in mind, as well as a tentative roadmap for progressively achieving their ultimate objectives. The roadmap helps to guide decision-making and suggests prudent steps toward the ultimate goal.

For organizations or businesses, positioning is especially critical, since an uncertain future may put the entire enterprise and its personnel in harm's way. A leader must understand the business model the organization needs and define it clearly. Due to constant fluctuating changes in the market, industry, and environment, the model must be agile and flexible enough to potentially improve the future or otherwise embrace it without major redirection. This is the hardest challenge, since no one should expect to be able to predict the future accurately. However, a leader should have a sound instinct and understand how to build an agile business model and a flexible foundation for coping with the unexpected, such as changing economic environments and/or governmental regulations, so that the enterprise will endure and continue to thrive.

Position: Levels of Effectiveness

Level One: Reactive. At Level One we have little sense of where we are and where we want to be. It's all about firefighting rather than planning for the future. We are frequently blindsided by change.

Level Two: Responsive. At Level Two we have a vision for the future and a plan for achieving it. We actively seek information on what's around the bend, and we respond quickly to change.

Level Three: Strategic. At Level Three we anticipate trends and prepare ourselves and our teams in advance. We develop a global, integrated roadmap to achieve our company's long-term vision. We are good at achieving the long-term vision by executing short-term steps that bring immediate benefit to the organization.

Position—Concrete Steps for Putting This Discipline into Action

Individual. As innovators, we need to crystallize our vision for the future and develop a strategic, step-by-step roadmap for achieving it, identifying the key milestones and deliverables along the way. We need to anticipate and incorporate expected changes and be flexible enough to respond to the unexpected. Positioning applies to our careers as well. We need to strive to beat deadlines and exceed goals. We should position ourselves for the future, new opportunities, and the next advancement with the right work experience and the right credentials.

Team and Organization. Teams and organizations must manage for the long term while delivering in the short term. Leaders must clearly define and communicate their vision and strategy and by doing so provide their teams with a future goal that can drive innovation throughout the organization. The creation of strategic business value is first and foremost.

The organization and its teams must be able to focus on the future, anticipating how it will unfold and developing plans accordingly. In some cases, we can forecast what will happen with some accuracy and draw our roadmap to account for them. In other cases, we can anticipate several likely scenarios without knowing what will really happen. In still others, something completely unpredictable and even game changing can happen. Agility and flexibility are the keys.

How to Position
- ✓ Position for tomorrow, not today
- ✓ Focus on creating strategic business value—understand the company or organization's vision and goals
- ✓ Position with a strategic view from a global perspective, and fully understand every country's local requirements for defining your roadmap
- ✓ Prepare a sound business case to ensure proper decision—demonstrate financial and business benefits
- ✓ Consider all possible creative ideas, not just the current way of doing business
- ✓ Exercise sound judgment in decision-making
- ✓ Leverage and collaborate broadly with people outside of your organization, worldwide, in different industries, and with different experience levels, to understand what might be available in the marketplace
- ✓ Position by focusing on your core business and leverage strategic partners with related core competencies
- ✓ The race is within yourself and your own organization for continuous improvements

提 Promote

One of the most overlooked and under-practiced disciplines that innovators must master is knowing how to create awareness, understanding, and appreciation for the value of their innovations and their brand.

Most people do not pay enough attention to promotion. However, this is the critical factor for acquiring support for internal funding and/or external capital investment. It is vital that innovators understand the value of more than just promotion in general. It is important to understand the techniques for successful and effective promotion at every stage of the innovation life cycle.

There are many areas to focus upon:

1. *Promotion materials*—An effective promotion is the ability to present our innovative ideas in business terms, with facts and data for a business case, highlighting the value to the business and its customers.
2. *Promotion style*—Good communication skills are critical. Our message must be clear and concise, in layman's language that everyone can understand. Keep it simple, with just enough information to deliver your message!
3. *Knowledge of both the subject and the market*—It is critical to compare any innovative ideas with what is already in the marketplace.
4. *Promotion at every stage of the life cycle*—Promotion is critical to acquire initial funding approval, then receive sustained strategic and execution plan support among all stakeholders, and—after execution—successfully compete for industry recognition and awards.

Promote: Levels of Effectiveness

Level One: Creates Uncertainty. At Level One we have little or no focus on ensuring the value and brand are clearly communicated. Instead, we create uncertainty about it. We fail to gain necessary buy-in and support. Nor are we able to achieve appropriate recognition of potential and actual benefits.

Level Two: Creates Understanding. At Level Two we are able to clearly communicate the value proposition and secure funding and buy-in. We use regular and reliable channels to build awareness, knowledge, and interest. We are deliberate about measuring and communicating results.

Level Three: Creates Excitement. Level Three people are master promoters who create buzz and ensure endorsement by appealing to the interests of others. We never assume the message is already out there or understood. We leverage every opportunity to educate others, and we generate interest and enthusiasm (e.g., elevator pitches, awards). We benchmark against industry and differentiate brand and strategic value as well as results.

Promote—Concrete Steps for Putting This Discipline into Action

Individuals. To promote ourselves and our work, we should learn to "blow our own horn," but in a way that cannot be mistaken as bragging. The most effective method is through metrics. As a matter of course, when we innovate, we should establish a baseline to which we reference and compare our new and improved results. In effect, we provide before and after pictures as a way of showing how our innovation is improving things.

We should always communicate our ideas—and our accomplishments—in terms of business value. What will our ideas gain, save, or achieve? When we answer these questions in our presentations, we earn the attention our audience, whether it be our company's decision makers, venture capitalists, or potential customers. Once an idea does become a project, we should develop a marketing and communications plan to support it.

Teams and Organizations. Teams and organizations, like individuals, should also be referencing metrics and business value in promoting their work. Teams can make a policy of promoting ideas and solutions through the lifecycle of their projects. First we promote in an effort to get funding and staff, then to garner support and buy-in, then to encourage awareness and interest. Finally, when our vision becomes reality, we promote to demonstrate the value and benefits of our work. Throughout, we should be thinking long term, but striving to deliver short-term benefits as early as possible—and promoting that fact.

Organizations can formalize a process where money is earmarked for limited initial funding of promising ideas, allowing teams to test assumptions and potential through smaller studies and experimentation. Ideas that prove promising can then move to another funded stage as the real costs and potential benefits become clear.

Organizations should encourage teams to benchmark and apply for industry awards and recognition. Both provide a great way to promote a company's innovation accomplishments and to motivate teams and individuals to even greater achievements.

How to Promote
✓ Promote with passion and energy. Passion is contagious
✓ Constantly assess each moment as an opportunity to promote
✓ Focus on promotional details—why, how, whom, when, where, and what to promote
✓ Create fact-based promotion. Benchmark against industry for recognition and awards
✓ Always have a three-minute elevator speech ready—simple and clear
✓ Promote widely. Never assume that people have already heard the message
✓ Promote your brand clearly based on delivering customer value and benefits, and make sure people understand its prospective value.
✓ Focus on the value to your customers' and users' business interests—not just your product's functions/features
✓ Everyone should acquire the skills for promotion

連 Connect

No one innovates alone. Innovation cannot exist in isolation. Innovators reach out across and beyond traditional boundaries to bring together the ideas, expertise, and experiences of diverse people, disciplines, solutions, and industries.

Connection is extremely important for both business and personal success. Innovators must have connections if their ideas are to be successfully funded and executed. There are several different focal points involved:

Connect with people diversely and globally–people do business with others they know and trust. Connect with people honestly and openly, with no immediate agenda. Connect for mutual interest and learning from each other, as well as to leverage from different perspectives.

Connect with business vision, goals, strategies, and plans. It is important to connect broadly while innovating. Innovative ideas must always target business success.

Connect: Levels of Effectiveness

Level One: Stand-Alone. At Level One we exhibit a silo-type mentality. We remain isolated in our thinking, approach, and solutions. We may go through the motions of collaboration, but often with the intent of just getting it over with. (We call that *clobberation*.) This leader is purely transaction-focused and has not understood the importance of relationship building.

Level Two: Integrated. At Level Two we are well connected, and before making decisions, we weigh a wide range of input from a diverse group of stakeholders. We align ourselves and our initiatives with corporate strategy, or with existing or planned solutions. We seek and unify stakeholder perspectives to ensure alliances and create effective solutions. This leader makes sure to invest in long-term relationships.

Level Three: Intersected. At Level Three we consistently reach outside of our usual "circle of connectivity" to find and leverage innovative ideas and new ways of creating business value. We actively seek out diverse and seemingly unconnected industries, age groups, technologies, and more. We enjoy helping others to succeed. This leader establishes enduring partnerships through integrity, trust, and generosity.

Connect—Concrete Steps for Putting This Discipline into Action

Individual. Establishing relationships and connections should be a part of everyone's everyday habit. It's as important as everything else we do on the job. They should never be sacrificed in the effort to make some particular task happen—by ignoring people in our haste, or humiliating them when we catch them in a mistake, or the hundred other ways we can be tempted to hurt people as we try to get a job done. In the end, those relationships and those people are what matter for the bigger picture, the big results we are looking for from our team—not to mention the positive effect on our lives and health when we work in harmony with others.

When focusing too narrowly on getting the task at hand completed—an issue of the moment—endangers a long-term relationship, we have to step back and restore our priorities. And while connections will occasionally be weakened by the stress associated with projects of great importance and the natural pressures of change, we should always take the high road of maintaining strong connection, rather than the low road of conflict.

Team and Organization. In addition to making personal connections, an innovation leader has to make sure that team members connect with one another, with the company at large, and with the world outside. The team leader can help develop internal connections by ensuring that team members understand the requirements of each corporate stakeholder, so that everyone can work together to reach the overall objectives, not just their individual pieces of the puzzle. Team and organizational leaders can help forge external connections by encouraging participation in industry events; ensuring close customer contact; and bringing in speakers, industry experts, partners, vendors, and others who can widen staff horizons.

We can also reexamine the prevailing system of rewards. Do incentives exist for team leaders to form working relationships with other teams? How about between business units? Can bonus systems be set up that reward, for example, sales growth throughout the organization rather than just in our own small groups? Finally, we must encourage an evaluation of values and character in the criteria for recruiting new employees. Many companies are already doing this.

How to Connect

✓ Connect globally, broadly across industries, institutions, organizations, and age groups

✓ Connect with strategy, systems, and processes, as well as with people

✓ Connect when you don't need a favor from people

✓ Connect strategically, not focused on immediate needs or transactions

✓ Connect openly, encouraging mutual trust and integrity

✓ Connect constantly, seizing every moment and every opportunity

✓ Connect with empathy—treat everyone as they personally wish to be treated

✓ Connect generously—do not be calculating constantly

✓ Connect is *not* taking advantage of people or using them for your benefit

✓ Help to connect other people together for their mutual benefit

✓ Help other people whenever you can, not only for your own immediate interests

✓ Connections require time-consuming efforts, so be patient

✓ Successful connections demand emotional intelligence on both sides

承 Commit

Successful innovators must take a personal "No Turning Back" approach that inspires others to participate, not recklessly, but with an emphasis on learning and necessary change, and without losing sight of the common goal.

Commitment involves determination, with a sense of responsibility and accountability. Innovators have to be "on a mission," totally laser-focused, and unwilling to let anyone stop them from pursuing their goals. Commitment is also not surrendering when confronted with challenges, but responding wisely. Innovators must be able to admit their mistakes and adjust their paths accordingly. Commitment requires persistence, a positive attitude, teamwork, and resourcefulness.

Commitment does not involve being inflexible, ignoring other people's suggestions or warnings, or refusing to adjust our course, if the original direction was not quite correct.

As an innovator, commitment means securing personal dedication and support from the team, our own organization, and—possibly—external investors. Responsibility for ensuring the delivery of successful innovative ideas that attract inside and/or outside investment is perhaps the greatest challenge.

Commit: Levels of Effectiveness

Level One: Avoids Risk. At Level One we are overly cautious about risking change in order to avoid "egg-on-the-face" issues. We don't differentiate between personal risk and business risk—it's all personal. Typically we add to—but do not change—as a way of hedging bets. We are unlikely to persevere in the face of great difficulty or impending "failure."

Level Two: Minimizes Risk. At Level Two we are willing to take a stand about what needs to change, and we set about changing it. But we are focused on minimizing risk rather than managing it. We recognize the roller-coaster life cycle of innovation projects and do not bail out when the going gets tough. We soldier through when obstacles appear—we don't retreat. We are decisive and accountable.

Level Three: Manages Risk. At Level Three we know how to manage business and financial risk, leveraging experimentation, fast-failure, and other strategies that significantly reduce it. Our risks are *calculated*, not avoided. We put ourselves on the line, carrying personal risk in a way that inspires others and makes others feel safe. We anticipate difficulties, and we under-commit while always trying to over-deliver.

Commit—Concrete Steps for Putting This Discipline into Action

Individual. As innovators, we commit to change by putting ourselves on the line. In effect, we have to stand up and say, "I think we can do this better, and this is the way I'd like to try." We don't have to bet our job or career every time we propose a new initiative, but we do have to make it clear that we're willing to take a calculated risk. Then we can better engage the support and commitment of our organization and the team on which we will rely.

Teams and Organizations. Teams and organizations commit to innovation by providing employees with a culture of safety that welcomes ideas and recognizes that not all of these ideas will pan out. This requires a shift in the processes, controls, and other cultural signals that shape behavior. Teams and organizations must recognize the types of results that their current practices reward and the types of failures that are penalized. Then they can redefine them to better support a culture of innovation. By changing these cultural signals and implementing clear guidelines and practices for managing innovation risks, funding, projects, and learning, teams and organizations demonstrate their own commitment to innovation.

How to Commit
- ✓ Passion creates commitment and persistence
- ✓ Commit wholeheartedly to the path you choose
- ✓ Commit wisely, with carefully calculated risks
- ✓ Commit and obtain buy-in from your team and organization

(continued)

- ✓ Commit funding, staffing, resources, support, P&L, and so forth
- ✓ Commit delivery of functions and features, and on a reasonable schedule
- ✓ Commit, but remember that it's better to under-promise and over-deliver than it is to over-promise
- ✓ Commit, but maintain an open mind. Always allow people to discuss issues and ideas
- ✓ Commit, but be flexible. Be aware of changes and unexpected events or incidents, which might require further consideration
- ✓ Commitment is not dictatorship

行 Execute

Innovators understand how to deliver value in the present, while paving a path to reach their future objective. They find their own way through experimentation and learning, and advance flawlessly. Innovators make progress themselves and simultaneously fuel progress for others.

Execute means making your vision a reality. It is extremely important to deliver tangible results. Vision is essential, but without execution, it is merely a daydream or vaporware. This is one of the most difficult hurdles along any innovator's journey. Many potential innovators are very creative, and they have wonderful ideas, but unfortunately many of them cannot make those ideas happen. It frequently takes a different set of skills and disciplines to become a leader proficient at delivering results. The desirable characteristics necessary to be good at executing plans and producing results flawlessly include: being laser-focused but flexible; having a positive attitude, tenacity, and a "never give up" approach; and encouraging teamwork and collaboration, as well as having good communications skills.

We talked a lot about flawless execution and zero-defect aspirations. There are business objectives and other initiatives that have zero tolerance for errors, just like the NASA Spaceflight projects and every-day airplane flights. The Six-Sigma approach is not good enough when our proper goal should be zero defects. There are proven ways to approach this level of excellence.

Execute: Levels of Effectiveness

Level One: Unproductive. As leaders at Level One, we aim too high or too low. We have difficulty defining or managing the scope of our projects. We tend to oversimplify or overcomplicate. We are rarely in touch with what's actually required by customers and clients. We get "stuck in the mud," unable to maintain focus to bring about desired results.

Level Two: Systematic. When we are operating at Level Two, we use a standard methodology to define and execute structured stages and to manage scope. We have a realistic understanding of what's required and how to get there. We always pilot to test our assumptions. We have developed and use effective project, budget, and issues management processes.

Level Three: Accelerated. At Level Three we are focused on creating demonstrable customer value with each stage. We remember to drive for the quickest wins that can stand on their own. We utilize rapid experimentation and fast failure techniques to test assumptions up front. Finally, we leverage metrics effectively to track, communicate and celebrate progress.

Execute—Concrete Steps for Putting This Discipline into Action

Individual. Innovators deal effectively with complexity through communication, teamwork, and planning, maintaining a dual focus on flawless execution and rapid value delivery. They work with their stakeholders to assess present positions, design practical solutions, and thoroughly understand the goals, quality requirements, and risks. They proceed in carefully scoped phases, structuring each one around the fastest, most achievable benefit that would be valued by the customer.

They leverage experimentation and incorporate the principles of "fail fast" to test and modify their assumptions and strategy. They look for metrics and other fact-based ways to measure and communicate progress, continually improving their approach and solution as they move forward.

Team and Organization. Teams and organizations can formalize processes that incorporate the principles of flawless execution and rapid value delivery. Each of these, of course, first requires that leaders set and communicate the standards for teams and projects. They can then employ practices such as change management reviews, which happen before project execution, and postmortem reviews, which happen afterwards. Change management reviews ensure that project plans account effectively for business and other risks. Postmortem reviews capture the lessons learned during the execution of a project. Teams can even have a "pre-postmortem" review session that involves imagining all of the things that might go wrong and then developing contingency plans accordingly.

How to Execute
✓ Make your vision a reality with determination
✓ Passion creates energy and positive attitude—never give up
✓ Maintain a "laser focus" upon delivery of results and commitment
✓ Assemble the best team with common goals and where everyone is "on a mission"
✓ Pursue "flawless execution"—raise the standards of excellence—always aspire to zero-defect execution
✓ Divide each project into smaller phases, with short-term achievable milestones
✓ Concentrate on key deliverables and circumvent any unexpected issues
✓ Always focus on the key goals—do not get distracted by less important issues

✓ Be flexible for unforeseen events—make sound judgment for alternatives

✓ Establish benchmarks both before and after each project and/or program

✓ Measure, communicate, and celebrate accomplishments immediately

變 Evolve

When companies achieve innovation as "business-as-usual," the search for improvement never ends. Innovators don't rest complacently on their laurels; they barely even glance at them. Change is hard, but constant change is harder. Innovators know the drill.

Evolve is, in effect, a constantly revolving life cycle of innovation. Innovators always look for new creative ideas, or they return to improve what they once did—only much better, faster, and cheaper.

"Change is the law of life. And those who look only to the past or present are certain to miss the future," President Kennedy once said. It is very easy to savor the accomplishments of the past and present, but it is even more exciting and enjoyable to continuously exceed what we have already done. As Tarkan Maner said, "the race is with yourself." We all should always compete against ourselves and what we have already done. This way, we will never be complacent. Leaders should inspire people and reward them for leading change and for a mentality of "timely obsolescent destruction."

This same concept applies to companies and organizations. If we race against ourselves, we will never stop racing, regardless of what our competitors are doing. With the passion and will to win, constantly exceeding ourselves will definitely achieve true business value and victories over the competition.

Evolve: Levels of Effectiveness

Level One: Satisfied. At Level One we are fully content with recent efforts and achievements and are enjoying a sense of completion and pride. We are feeling comfortable and secure with the company's current strategic and competitive position and the role we've played in both.

Level Two: Pacing. At Level Two we are pleased with recent efforts and achievements but are open to ongoing change and improvement. We are continually monitoring the company's strategic and competitive position and remain alert for the need to make changes.

Level Three: Driving. At Level Three we've already moved on! We are actively seeking and implementing change and improvement. We are making a major impact on the company recognizing that innovation should be a part of every business process. We are continually seeking ways to enhance strategic value and improve our competitive position.

Evolve—Concrete Steps for Putting This Discipline into Action

Individual. Continual innovation for the individual means producing results and celebrating success, yet never allowing ourselves to be content with what we have achieved. We can maintain a mind-set of "the best is yet to come" and constantly search out ways to be better. This applies to how we respond to adversity as well. We always stay positive and do not waste time on things we cannot control. Innovators don't defend themselves against opportunities to learn; they seek them out.

Team and Organization. Teams often bond around the great accomplishments that they produce, yet this bonding can produce a new and rigid status quo. The role of the team leader, therefore, is critical. We have to be open to suggestions for doing things differently, reward questions as much as answers, and encourage new ideas; in so doing, we continually encourage the team to move forward and out of its comfort zone.

An organization's culture should be one that inspires and encourages people to continually innovate. This requires executive focus and structured processes that continually examine existing solutions and challenge people to think about ways to improve them. The organization should implement practices that instill and/or reinforce the idea of "innovation-as-usual."

How to Evolve
- ✓ "The important race is always with yourself" (Tarkan Maner)
- ✓ Inspire and create a culture of continuous improvement—maintain your momentum
- ✓ Never become complacently satisfied with your prior successes
- ✓ Rotate people through different assignments to continually challenge them with fresh perspectives
- ✓ Always look for the next new ideas and opportunities for continuous improvement
- ✓ Uncover and evaluate strategic future plans, from all available sources—suppliers, vendors, partners, venture capitalists, startups, and the like
- ✓ To remain competitive, you need to continuously evolve
- ✓ Reward people for continuous innovation and creating business value
- ✓ Measure and communicate loudly and broadly for results from designed destruction
- ✓ "The Best Is Yet to Come"

Appendix II

Biographies of Individuals Interviewed for This Book

Tenley E. Albright, MD

Director, MIT Collaborative Initiatives
Massachusetts Institute of Technology

Dr. Albright is the director of MIT Collaborative Initiatives, which promotes a systems-based approach to solving deep-rooted societal issues by engaging experts from a broad range of disciplines both within and outside the scope of a problem.

She is a faculty member and lecturer in general surgery at Harvard Medical School, is currently on the Board of Research!America and the Bloomberg Family Foundation, and is a consultant to, and formerly chairwoman of the Board of Regents of the National Library of Medicine at the National Institutes of Health. Dr. Albright also serves on the National Council of Advisors of the Center of the Study of the Presidency and Congress. She was formerly a director of West Pharmaceutical Services, Inc., State Street Bank and Trust Company, and the Whitehead Institute for Biomedical Research. She has also served as delegate to the World Health Assembly for four years and has been inducted into the Military Health System Honor Society. Dr. Albright is the recipient of the 2011 White House Fellows Valenti Award.

Dr. Albright graduated from Harvard Medical School after attending Radcliffe College and has received eight honorary degrees. Earlier, she was a gold medal–winning Olympic figure skater.

Deborah Ancona

Seley Distinguished Professor of Management
Professor of Organization Studies
Director, MIT Leadership Center
MIT Sloan School of Management

Deborah Ancona's pioneering research into how successful teams operate has highlighted the critical importance of managing outside, as well as inside, the team's boundary. This research directly led to the concept of X-Teams as a vehicle for driving innovation within large organizations. Her work also focuses on the concept of distributed leadership and on the development of research-based tools, practices, and teaching/coaching models that enable organizations to foster creative leadership at every level.

She is the author of the book *X-Teams: How to Build Teams That Lead, Innovate, and Succeed* (Harvard Business School Press, June 2007) and the related article, "In Praise of the Incomplete Leader" (*Harvard Business Review*, Feb. 2007). In addition to *X-Teams*, her studies of team performance also have been published in the *Administrative Science Quarterly*, the *Academy of Management Journal*, *Organization Science*, and the *Sloan Management Review*. Her previous book, *Managing for the Future: Organizational Behavior and Processes* (South-Western College Publishing, 1999, 2005), centers on the skills and processes needed in today's diverse and changing organization. Dr. Ancona has served as a consultant on leadership and innovation to companies such as AT&T, BP, Credit Suisse First Boston, Hewlett-Packard, Merrill Lynch, News Corporation, and Vale.

Dr. Ancona holds a B.A. and an M.S. in psychology from the University of Pennsylvania and a Ph.D. in management from Columbia University.

Eugene Y. Chan, MD

Founder, President, and Chief Scientific Officer, DNA Medicine Institute

Dr. Chan is a physician-innovator who has made numerous contributions to genomic technologies, medical devices, and instrumentation. He is the founder, president, and chief scientific officer of the DNA Medicine Institute, an organization focused on advancing patient care, alleviating human suffering, and treating disease through innovation. His current work is focused on developing a small handheld device that will allow anyone to perform hundreds of lab tests on a single drop of blood. This technology was recently successfully tested with NASA in zero gravity. He is also developing a noninvasive diagnostic device for malaria, which will allow for improved diagnosis and management of this disease in global health settings. Eugene graduated from Harvard University *summa cum laude* and the Harvard Medical School, MIT HST program with honors. He completed his postgraduate medical training in internal medicine at Harvard Medical School's Brigham and Women's Hospital. While taking a six-year hiatus from medical school, he founded and served as the chairman and CEO of U.S. Genomics, now Pathogenetix. Its technology is being utilized for diagnosing complex infectious diseases without the need for blood cultures. He is the founder of five biotechnology and medical-related companies that have raised more than $125 million in funding and launched numerous successful products. He holds more than 40 U.S., world, issued, and pending patents. He has been recognized as one of *Esquire* magazine's "Best and Brightest" and *MIT Technology Review*'s "Top 100 Innovators Under 35." His work has been praised in the pages of *Fortune, Forbes, Newsweek, Wired, Scientific American*, and the *New York Times*.

Gerald Chertavian

Founder and CEO, Year Up

Gerald Chertavian is the founder of Year Up, an innovative program that empowers urban young adults to enter the economic mainstream. With an annual operating budget of more than $60 million, Year Up is one of the fastest growing nonprofits in the nation and was recognized by *Fast Company* and The Monitor Group as one of the top 25 organizations using business excellence to engineer social change. Gerald has received numerous awards and honorary degrees for social entrepreneurship and youth development, and his work has been featured in the *New York Times*, *USA Today*, *Newsweek*, *The NewsHour with Jim Lehrer*, and *Fox Business*. He serves on the Massachusetts State Board of Elementary and Secondary Education and the Board of Advisors for the Harvard Business School Social Enterprise Initiative and recently led a working session at the first Clinton Global Initiative to focus solely on driving economic growth in America. A graduate of Bowdoin College and Harvard Business School, Gerald lives in Boston with his wife and three children. His book, *A Year Up*, is a *New York Times* bestseller.

Dean Kamen

Founder and President, DEKA Research & Development Corporation

Dean Kamen is an inventor, an entrepreneur, and an advocate for science and technology. He holds more than 440 U.S. and foreign patents, many of them for innovative medical devices that have expanded the frontiers of health care worldwide. While still a college undergraduate, he invented the first wearable infusion pump. In 1976, he founded his first medical device company, AutoSyringe, Inc., to manufacture and market the pumps.

Following the sale of AutoSyringe, Inc., he founded DEKA Research & Development Corporation to develop internally generated inventions as well as to provide research and development for major corporate clients. Examples of technologies developed by

DEKA include the HomeChoice™ portable dialysis machine, the iBOT™ Mobility System, the Segway™ Human Transporter, a DARPA-funded robotic arm, a new and improved Stirling engine, and the Slingshot water purifier.

Mr. Kamen has received many awards for his efforts, including the National Medal of Technology in 2000 and the Lemelson–MIT Prize in 2002. He was inducted into the National Inventors Hall of Fame in 2005 and has been a member of the National Academy of Engineering since 1997.

In addition to DEKA, one of Mr. Kamen's proudest accomplishments is founding *FIRST®* (For Inspiration and Recognition of Science and Technology), an organization dedicated to motivating the next generation to understand, use, and enjoy science and technology. Founded in 1989, this year *FIRST* will serve more than 300,000 young people, ages 6 to 18, in more than 50 countries around the globe. High school–aged participants are eligible to apply for more than $15 million in scholarships from leading colleges, universities, and corporations.

Tarkan Maner

Ex-President & CEO Wyse Technology

Global executive operator, investor, and advisor in Information Technology. Operational and investment areas of focus include information security, infrastructure management, social media, mobility, virtualization, converged infrastructures, contextual intelligence, and cloud computing technologies. Executive roles at Dell, Wyse, CA, IBM, Quest, and Sterling Software. Founding chairman of TechAmerica's state and local government cloud computing commission. Served, serve and serving on the boards of the Bay Area Council, World Economic Forum's Cyber-Security Alliance, Silicon Valley Education Foundation, and Silicon Valley Leadership Group, a coalition of senior executives to improve the quality of life for all citizens of the region and the world through its advocacy around public and private policy issues, from the mecca of innovation and progress, Silicon Valley. Involved in leading, advising, and fund-raising for several not-for-profit organizations and programs around economic development, poverty elimination, entrepreneurship, education, and social justice, including E&Y Entrepreneurship, Strategic Growth and Innovation Programs, MIT's Collaborative Initiatives, Network for Teaching Entrepreneurship (NFTE), Project Skolkovo (Russia), and eLearning Africa. Advisor to several IT start-up companies and boards. The Winner of 2012 E&Y Entrepreneur of the Year Award in California; a frequent speaker, commentator, and author on current business, economic, and social issues in the media and academic circles. Graduated from Istanbul Technical University in Turkey with a B.S. degree in Engineering Management. Received an MBA degree at Midwestern State University, in Wichita Falls, Texas, in the heartland of America. Attended Advanced Management Program at Harvard Business School along with several business and political leaders of today. Avid fan of sports, politics, arts, books, nature, history, Earth, innovative ideas, and people.

More on Tarkan at: www.tarkanmaner.com.

Tom Mendoza

Vice Chairman, NetApp

Tom joined NetApp in 1994 and was responsible for sales until becoming president in 2000. In 2009 he became vice chairman.

Tom has given talks on the power of corporate culture and leadership all over the world to people in such diverse organizations as the U.S. Marine Corps, West Point, CIO forums, Oracle's Leaders Circle, and Stanford University. In 2009 he was the corecipient with NetApp Chairman Dan Warmenhoven of the Morgan Stanley Leadership Award for Global Commerce.

Tom holds a B.A. degree from the University of Notre Dame and is an alumnus of Stanford University's Executive Business Program. In September 2000, Notre Dame renamed its business school the Mendoza College of Business after an endowment made by Tom and Kathy Mendoza.

Admiral Michael Mullen

Admiral Mike Mullen served as the 17th Chairman of the Joint Chiefs of Staff (2007–2011). He was the principal military advisor to

President George W. Bush and President Barack Obama, as well as two Secretaries of Defense.

He led the military during a critical period of transition, concluding the combat mission in Iraq and creating a new military strategy for Afghanistan. He advocated for the rapid development and fielding of innovative technologies, championed emerging and enduring international partnerships, and advanced new methods for combating terrorism.

Admiral Mullen has deep experience in leading change in complex organizations, executive development and succession planning, diversity implementation, crisis management, strategic planning, budget policy, congressional relations, risk management, technical innovation, and cyber security. Widely recognized as an "honest broker" in his key leadership roles as a trusted advisor to both President Bush and President Obama, he also maintains strong relationships with leaders around the globe.

He and his wife, Deborah, remain staunch advocates for disabled veterans and their families, drawing public attention and institutional focus on a broad range of challenging issues.

A native of Los Angeles, Admiral Mullen graduated from the U.S. Naval Academy in 1968. His extensive naval fleet command experience, progressing through every level—and including NATO—culminated in his appointment as the 28th Chief of Naval Operations (2005–2007).

Admiral Mullen earned an MS in Operations Research from the Naval Postgraduate School and completed the Advanced Management Program at the Harvard Business School.

Nathan Myhrvold

Founder, Intellectual Ventures

Nathan Myhrvold founded Intellectual Ventures after retiring as chief strategist and chief technology officer of Microsoft Corporation.

During his 14 years at Microsoft, Dr. Myhrvold founded Microsoft Research and numerous technology groups. Dr. Myhrvold is an avid inventor who has been awarded hundreds of patents and has hundreds of patents pending.

Before joining Microsoft, he was a postdoctoral fellow in the department of applied mathematics and theoretical physics at Cambridge University and worked with Professor Stephen Hawking. Dr. Myhrvold earned a doctorate in theoretical and mathematical physics and a master's degree in mathematical economics from Princeton University, and a master's degree in geophysics and space physics and a bachelor's degree in mathematics from UCLA.

An avid nature and wildlife photographer, Dr. Myhrvold's work is featured in the books *America 24/7* and *Washington 24/7*, where his photographs helped capture a week in the life of people and nature in the United States during the spring of 2003. His research has been published in scientific journals including *Science, Nature, Paleobiology, Environmental Research Letters, Journal of Vertebrate Paleontology* and the *Physical Review*, and he has contributed articles to magazines and online news sites including *Harvard Business Review, The Wall Street Journal, Fortune, Time, Bloomberg BusinessWeek* and *National Geographic Traveler*. In 2004, he provided the foreword to a book profiling some of the world's greatest inventors—*Juice: The Creative Fuel That Drives World-Class Inventors*. He has also been named one of the most influential people in intellectual property by several leading IP trade publications.

Last year he released the award-winning *Modernist Cuisine: The Art and Science of Cooking*, a cookbook surveying the science, technology, and techniques used in modern cuisine. The James Beard Foundation honored *Modernist Cuisine* with awards for Cookbook of the Year and Cooking from a Professional Point Of View. In 2012, he released the highly acclaimed *Modernist Cuisine at Home*.

Samuel J. Palmisano

CEO, IBM 2002–2011

From January 1, 2003, through December 31, 2011, Mr. Palmisano served as chairman, president, and CEO of IBM. He was chairman of the Board from January through September 2012. Under his leadership, IBM achieved record financial performance, transformed itself into a globally integrated enterprise, and introduced its Smarter Planet agenda.

Mr. Palmisano began his career with IBM in 1973 in Baltimore, Maryland. In a 39-year career with the company, he held leadership positions that included senior vice president and group executive of the Personal Systems Group, senior vice president and group executive of IBM Global Services, senior vice president and group executive of Enterprise Systems, and president and chief operating officer.

Mr. Palmisano is a graduate of The Johns Hopkins University. Among his many business accomplishments, Mr. Palmisano was awarded an Honorary Degree of Doctor of Humane Letters from Johns Hopkins University in 2012 and from Rensselaer Polytechnic Institute in 2005. In 2006, he was awarded an Honorary Fellowship from the London Business School. Mr. Palmisano has received a number of business awards, including the Atlantic Council's Distinguished Business Leadership Award in 2009 and the inaugural Deming Cup, presented in 2010 by the W. Edwards Deming Center for Quality, Productivity, and Competitiveness at Columbia Business School. He is also an elected member of the American Academy of Arts and Sciences and served as co-chair of the Council on Competitiveness's National Innovation Initiative.

James S. Phalen

Head of Global Operation and Technology
State Street Corporation

James S. Phalen is an executive vice president and head of Global Operation and Technology. He is also a member of State Street's Management Committee, the company's most senior strategy and policy-making team.

Previously, Mr. Phalen was head of State Street's international operations for investment servicing and investment research and trading. In this role, he oversaw strategy, operations, and business development for State Street's investment services and investment research and trading outside North America.

He was formerly chairman and CEO of CitiStreet, one of the largest global benefits delivery firms in the country. Before joining CitiStreet, Mr. Phalen spent eight years in senior roles at State

Street. Prior to this, he was president and chief operating officer of Boston Financial (BFDS), a joint venture of State Street and DST Systems, Inc.

Mr. Phalen is a director of Boston Financial Data Services and the Boston Medical Center. He holds a degree from Boston College and graduated from the Stonier Graduate School of Banking. He also attended the Executive Development Program at Massachusetts Institute of Technology's Sloan School of Management.

Linda S. Sanford

Senior Vice President, Enterprise Transformation, IBM

Linda Sanford leads the strategy for IBM's internal transformation to becoming the premier globally integrated, smarter enterprise. In this role, Ms. Sanford is responsible for working across IBM to transform core business processes, create an IT infrastructure to support and integrate processes globally, and help create a culture that fosters innovation.

Previously Ms. Sanford has held a number of senior leadership positions at IBM, including heading the Storage Systems Group, Global Industries and the mainframe division. Ms. Sanford is a member of the Women in Technology International Hall of Fame and the National Academy of Engineering.

Ms. Sanford coauthored *Let Go To Grow: Escaping the Commodity Trap*, a book that details how successful companies are pursuing strategies to drive long-term growth and innovation.

A graduate of St. John's University, Ms. Sanford earned an MS in Operations Research from Rensselaer Polytechnic Institute and was awarded an honorary doctorate in commercial science from St. John's.

John Swainson

President, Dell Software

In his role as Dell Software's president, John Swainson is responsible for building software capabilities and providing greater innovation and organizational support in the delivery of end-to-end IT solutions to Dell customers. The Software group adds to Dell enterprise solutions capabilities, accelerates profitable growth, and further differentiates the company by increasing its solutions portfolio with Dell-owned intellectual property.

Prior to joining Dell in 2012, Mr. Swainson was senior advisor to Silver Lake, a global private equity firm, and sat on a number of boards, including Broadcom, Assurant, Cadence Design Systems, and Serena Software. From early 2005 to the end of 2009, he was CEO and director of CA Technologies, a Fortune 500 enterprise software company.

Before joining CA Technologies, Mr. Swainson worked for IBM for more than 26 years, where he held various management positions in the United States and Canada, including seven years as general manager of the Application Integration Middleware Division, a business he founded in 1997. During that period, he and his team developed the WebSphere family of middleware products and Eclipse open source tools. He also led the IBM worldwide software sales organization and held numerous senior leadership roles in engineering, marketing, and sales management.

Mr. Swainson earned a bachelor's degree in engineering from the University of British Columbia, Canada. He currently serves on the board of Visa Inc., where he is the lead director.

John Thompson

CEO, Virtual Instruments
Instruments Board of Directors since 2009

Prior to joining Virtual Instruments, Mr. Thompson was chairman of the board and CEO of Symantec Corporation, the leader in Internet security, from April 1999 to April 2009. He continued to serve as chairman of the board until October 2011. Mr. Thompson also served in a number of senior leadership roles at IBM Corporation, including general manager of IBM Americas, prior to assuming the CEO role at Symantec. During his 10-year tenure as CEO of Symantec, Mr. Thompson transformed the company into a leader in security, storage, and systems management solutions, delivering world-class products to a global customer base, from individual consumers to many of the world's largest enterprises. He helped grow revenues from $600 million to more than $6 billion in ten years.

Beyond his role at Symantec, Mr. Thompson has served on the National Infrastructure Advisory Committee (NIAC), making recommendations regarding the security of nation's critical infrastructure, and the Financial Crisis Inquiry Commission, investigating the cause of the 2008 financial collapse and making recommendations to Congress on steps to avoid or mitigate the impact of a reoccurrence. He is an active investor in early-stage companies and currently serves on the board of directors of Liquid Robotics, the world's first wave-powered autonomous platform, and DOMO, an emerging platform for business intelligence. Mr. Thompson also serves on the board of UPS, the global leader in logistics, and Microsoft, the world's largest software company.

John W. Thompson completed his undergraduate studies at Florida A&M University and holds a master's degree in Management from MIT's Sloan School of Management.

Ming Tsai

Chef and Restaurant Owner

Ming Tsai is the James Beard Award–winning chef/owner of two restaurants—Blue Ginger and Blue Dragon. Also an Emmy Award winner, Mr. Tsai hosts PBS-TV's *Simply Ming*, now in its tenth season. Mr. Tsai is the author of five cookbooks, including his latest, *Simply Ming in Your Kitchen*.

In 2012, Mr. Tsai was invited by Secretary of State Hillary Clinton to represent the United States with the Diplomatic Culinary Partnership Initiative/American Chef Corps. The Chef Corps is a network of American chefs that participate with official government programs that use food as a foundation for international diplomacy efforts.

Mr. Tsai is a national spokesperson for the Food Allergy and Anaphylaxis Network (FAAN). Mr. Tsai also worked with Massachusetts Legislature to help write Bill S. 2701, which requires local restaurants to comply with food allergy awareness guidelines.

A member of the Harvard School of Public Health's Nutrition Round Table, Mr. Tsai also supports many charities, including Big Brothers Big Sisters, Cam Neely Foundation, Family Reach Foundation, and Greater Boston Food Bank.

About the Author

Madge M. Meyer—a public speaker, author, and the founder of Madge Meyer Consulting, LLC—is known for her unique yet practical approach to advancing innovation and leadership across organizations.

Madge was the Chief Innovation Officer and Technology Fellow at State Street Corporation, where she served as Executive Vice President for over a decade. During the past year, she represented State Street as a consultant, assisting MIT Collaborative Initiatives to bring innovative solutions to problems broadly ranging from global sustainability to health, education, and veterans' reintegration.

Madge has been recognized with twelve awards for her industry and community achievements, including *Bank Systems & Technology* "Elite 8 Innovators" and *Bank Technology News* "10th Annual Innovators List," which both honor executives who leverage innovation for competitive advantage. She was recently initiated, as a Simmons School of Management 2013 Chapter Honoree, into the International Beta Gamma Sigma Honor Society, as a leader in business and management, possessing and supporting the values of BGS. Madge's teams at State

Street were also recognized with thirty-two awards for innovation and excellence, including twelve IT environmental sustainability honors.

Prior to joining State Street, Madge served as first vice president for Merrill Lynch's Enterprise Technology Services. Earlier in her career, she was a scientific programmer working for IBM on the NASA Gemini Orbital Spaceflights. Later, she advanced through several executive positions at IBM with responsibilities for information technology and telecommunications

Madge is a graduate in mathematics and chemistry from the University of Mary-Hardin Baylor, and was commemorated as the 2010 Honoree on their College of Business Wall of Fame. She continued graduate study in Mathematics at St. Louis University. She currently serves on the board of the Wall Street Technology Association, is a Sierra Ventures CIO Advisory Board member, a member of Simmons College's School of Management Business Advisory Council, a CIO Advisory Board member of Globespan, an Advisory Board member of the Asian American Civic Association, and a member of the DNA Medicine Institute Business Advisory Board.

Madge believes passionately in making innovation "Business-as-Usual"—continually developing and implementing new ideas or solutions that create business value and increase competitive advantage.

Index